JOHN SAYWELL is a member of the Department of History at York University. He is the editor of the *Canadian Annual Review of Politics and Public Affairs.*

One of Canada's leading historians and political commentators traces the evolution of the Parti québécois from 1967 to 1976. This account, collected from yearly political surveys originally published in the *Canadian Annual Review* between 1967 and 1975, provides a complete and objective narrative of the party's history and its context in Quebec politics and society.

Professor Saywell draws the story together with an introduction, a linking narrative, and a final chapter on 1976 and the events surrounding the party's stunning victory in the November election.

Professor Saywell presents the history of the Parti québécois as it happened in a book that will interest all concerned with the destiny of Quebec and Canada.

JOHN SAYWELL

The Rise of the Parti Québécois 1967-76

UNIVERSITY OF TORONTO PRESS
Toronto and Buffalo

© 1977 University of Toronto Press
Toronto and Buffalo
Printed in Canada

Canadian Cataloguing in Publication Data

Saywell, John T., 1929–
    The rise of the Parti québécois, 1967–1976

Originally published in the Canadian Annual Review,
1967-1970, and the Canadian Annual Review of
politics and public affairs, 1971–1976.
ISBN 0-8020-2275-8 bd. ISBN 0-8020-6317-9 pa.

1. Parti québécois. 2. Quebec (Province) – Politics
and government – 1960–   I. Title
JL259.A56S39   329.9'714   C77-001160-8

The cartoons on pages 10, 22, 34, and 59 are reprinted with
permission of The Toronto Star.

This book has been published during the
Sesquicentennial year of the University of Toronto

Preface

In assembling this history of the Parti québécois from the *Canadian Annual Review* I have left the account of each year just as it was written. There is a value in a record as it happened, as it seemed to contemporaries with the evidence they had before them and who lacked the sometimes dubious benefit of hindsight. The very brief introductions to each year are designed simply to place the developments within the PQ in context. I would like to thank Susan Merry, the editorial assistant on the CAR, and Jock Bryce for their generous assistance in pulling this together and working on the events of 1976 at a time of year when serious pursuits are supposed to give way to merriment.

John Saywell
December 26,1976

The *Canadian Annual Review* has been published by University of Toronto Press since 1960 under the continuous editorial direction of John Saywell; he himself has written the annual accounts of politics in Quebec. The many quotations from French documents and editorials have been been translated for this work by Richard Howard, and some minor editorial alterations have been made to the original texts for the sake of consistency.

Contents

THE RISE OF THE PARTI QUÉBÉCOIS

Prologue

On November 15, 1976, the province of Quebec elected a government committed to achieving the political independence of Quebec. Separatism had always existed as an ideal for many and as an option for some; for Quebec had never rested easily within the framework of Canadian federalism or on the foundations of a predominantly anglophone, if not anglo-saxon, country. It was not until the 1960s, however, that Canadians had to deal with the idea of independence as a reality. The bombs, violence, and murders of the Front de Libération du Québec (FLQ) and other terrorist groups attracted the most attention, but the revolutionaries were less a danger to the country than the gradual movement of many politically active Quebeckers toward some form of semi-independent status. Most tried to define a new position for Quebec within the federal system; others boldly crossed the separatist boundary. Not until 1967, however, did they have a leader who was able to turn an idea – or a conviction – into a political party.

The catalyst in the movement for independence was René Lévesque. Without him it is unlikely that November 15 would have happened – certainly not as early as 1976. Not only did Lévesque ensure high visibility and credibility to the movement for independence, but he also had earned, in Quebec and across Canada, a reputation as a sound and progressive politician. In less than ten years he had built a party that could appear as a real, indeed the only, alternative to the Liberal government of Robert Bourassa. It was a remarkable accomplishment.

René Lévesque was born in the Gaspé in 1922, the son of a lawyer,

and grew up in a bilingual community. Some of his earliest recollec-
tions were of linguistic and religious differences and inequalities, and
his education in the seminary reflected the nationalist currents of the
1930s. In an article he wrote on 'la fête de Dollard' for the seminary
student paper *L'Envol* in 1936 he touched all the traditional bases of
French-Canadian national feeling – French origin, the 'glorious
annals' of history, language and religion, the struggle for survival, and
the 'mission of our race.' But then, almost apologetically, he turned to
'very prosaic' matters: 'In our country, we French Canadians are losing enormous sums in all the areas of trade, finance, industry and administration. Let us look to our pride and claim from the foreigners ...
instead of the contemptible positions we have now, the high offices
that are our due; let us claim them and know how to reach them. On
the day we have done that we will be able to call ourselves our own
masters, but not until that day.

'Verdict: let us encourage always, with all our might, the enlight-
ened patriots who watch over and defend our interests, for on their
labours depends the future of our race in America' (quoted in *Le
Devoir*, December 7, 1976).

Expelled for flunking math from the Jesuit college where he had en-
rolled when his widowed mother moved to Quebec in 1938, Lévesque
went to Laval and completed his baccalaureate in 1941. In the fall he
entered law school, where not only did he find the law uninteresting
but he found broadcasting far more exciting. As a youth he had always wanted to be a writer or a journalist, and finally in December
1943 he dropped out of law school determined to become a writer.
However, in the winter of 1943 it was much more likely that he would
become a soldier. But before the Canadian army beckoned, a friend
found him a position with the American Office of War Information and
he spent the rest of the war in England and France as a broadcaster
and interpreter with the American army.

Returning to Canada he joined the CBC's International Service. His
reputation as a broadcaster was established by his coverage of the
Korean war, after which he became director of Radio Canada's news
service. In 1956 he decided to freelance and soon launched 'Point de
Mire' ('Target') a television programme that was to make him
Quebec's best-known and most outspoken broadcaster. When the
producers on the French network went on strike in December 1958
René Lévesque was soon playing a leading role in the agitation. Before the strike ended in March, he had concluded that the stubborn

refusal of the federal minister of labour and Prime Minister Diefen-
baker to intervene and the apparent indifference, if not the hostility, of
the CBC management in Ottawa revealed a deep-seated cultural bias.
As he wrote in *Le Devoir* on March 11:

'Many, many weeks back, some people said that a racial cry was being raised, when it was advanced that a prolonged strike could mean
ruin or at least serious damage to a valuable public property of French
Canada. So a lot of us stopped saying that truth as we saw it.

'Now most of the damage has been done. CBC's higher-ups have run
the gamut from corporate irresponsibility to anonymous viciousness.
Cabinet ministers have stood up in the House like knights in incredible
armors of denseness, small-town vanity and brutal indifference.

'Some of us, maybe a lot of us, will come out of this permanently
disgusted with a certain ideal called National Unity. Never before have
we felt that apart from pleas every four years in painful 'political
French' National Unity is something designed almost exclusively to
keep negligible minorities nice and quiet.

'Never before we have felt that our affairs are bound to be either
tragically or comically mismanaged, as long as they remain in the
hands of men who have no understanding of them and make it quite
clear that they don't consider such lack as any kind of personal flaw.

'Some of us, and maybe many, come out of this with a tired and un-
worthy feeling that if such a strike had happened on English CBC, it
would – as the hon. George Nowlan said, and on this occasion not er-
roneously – have lasted no more than half an hour. To this day, ours
has lasted 66 days. Of such signal advantages is the privilege of being
French made up in this country!'(quoted in Jean Provencher, *René
Lévesque – Portrait of a Québécois* (Toronto 1975), 116-17).

The strike was a critical stage in the nationalist politicization of
René Lévesque. During the agitation he had worked with Jean Marchand and Gérard Pelletier, and afterwards he began to participate in
political discussions with a group to which they, and Pierre Trudeau,
belonged. Although members of the group were not Liberals – many
of them indeed were far to the left of the Liberals – they were attempting to help reshape the provincial Liberal party into a progressive alternative to the tottering goverment of Maurice Duplessis and the Union Nationale. As the 1960 election approached, Jean Lesage, the
Liberal leader, invited members of the group to become candidates.
After lengthy discussions, only René Lévesque decided to take the
plunge. (Ironically, three of the others were to move to Ottawa five

years later to stem the tide of nationalism that Lévesque was to help unleash.) Lévesque played a role second only to Jean Lesage in the campaign, and became minister of hydraulic resources and of public works in the Liberal cabinet.

Lévesque did not fit easily into a ministerial or Liberal harness. He much preferred the stump or the newsroom to the Assembly, and while his charm could be disarming his speeches and conversation were often marked by a bluntness foreign to most politicians. Moreover, even generously discounting his hyperbole, it soon became clear that he stood well to the left of his party and advocated a far greater role for the state in Quebec than his colleagues. It was Lévesque who persuaded – or compelled – the cabinet to nationalize the hydro-electric companies and it was he, more than Jean Lesage, who was identified as the spirit behind the *'Maîtres chez nous'* appeal in the 1962 election.

By then René Lévesque had decided that Canadian federalism had to be altered to accommodate the new Quebec he was helping to shape. Confederation was simply an experiment, he observed, which 'if the necessary adjustments' were not made would 'simply fail.' Before a largely anglophone student audience in 1961 he declared 'we have no real need of you as a group. The great threat to Confederation lies in the fact that – to take myself as an example – I am only interested in it out of a sense of obligation rather than real concern, and believe me, many French Canadians share this attitude.'

As the first terrorist bombs exploded in the streets of Montreal in 1963 and the reign of terror began that was to find its climax in the tragic days of October 1970, and as Jean Lesage declared war on the federal government's intransigence over tax sharing, René Lévesque's position became more sharply defined and his tone shriller. 'There must be a new Canada within a few years or Quebec will quit Confederation,' he told a Toronto audience. 'As for me, first and foremost I am a Québécois and second – with a rather growing doubt – a Canadian.' In Ottawa Prime Minister Pearson pinned his faith on the Royal Commission on Bilingualism and Biculturalism, but in Quebec Lévesque ridiculed the idea: 'There are two separate cultures, and it is impossible to merge them into one.'

By May 1964 as the Army for the Liberation of Quebec joined the FLQ in the streets and Premier Lesage pressed for an undefined 'special status,' his irrepressible and outspoken colleague had concluded that only the status of an associate state was acceptable:

Quebec is suffocating within the confines of an outmoded, obsolete Confederation, and the status quo is untenable now that Quebec has merely finished surviving and knows it can live a full life. Therefore, either Quebec will become an associate state within Canada, with a status guaranteeing it the economic, political and cultural powers necessary for its growth as a nation, or else Quebec will become independent, free to choose its own destiny within the limits, of course, imposed by the interdependence of nations in the twentieth century.' (quoted in Provencher, *Lévesque,* 205). The new status, he told a student audience in Montreal, should be negotiated 'as far as possible without guns and dynamite ... But if Quebec is denied this status, we shall have to separate.'

The *Montreal Star* warned on May 12, 1964, that Lévesque 'is not what many people believe he is, the tough, essentially responsible minister who gets carried away and says violent, pro-separatist things he later regrets. During the past year all his homework, all his visions, have been in terms of a separate Quebec ... He has begun to present a moral problem to his colleagues. Are they with him or against him?' The *Winnipeg Free Press* (May 25) declared that 'at some point Mr Lesage must take an unequivocal stand on the simple question of whether Quebec is to remain in Confederation or leave it. If he stands for Confederation as he seems to stand then Mr Lévesque must capitulate or resign ... Should Mr Lévesque succeed ... Mr Lesage will become the Kerensky of his Quebec Revolution.' French-Canadian editors had a greater tolerance for ambiguity, but Vincent Prince urged Mr Lévesque to take time out to write a speech, while Claude Ryan wrote in *Le Devoir* that the minister was 'a genuine enigma for English Canada. If he continues to babble as he now does, he will soon become the same for French Canadians.'

Clearly Lévesque was leaving his colleagues behind, although it was not easy to determine how far his associate state would differ from Jean Lesage's new federal system where Quebec would have control of 'all the economic, social, administrative and political levers thanks to which, and thanks only to which, it will be possible to realize the legitimate aspirations of an adult people.'

By 1965 Pierre Trudeau, en route to Ottawa and 24 Sussex Drive, had concluded that advocates of an associate state or special status were 'those who do not feel capable of saying they are separatists and carrying their thinking to its logical conclusion.' Mr Trudeau was more noted for his relentless logic than was the Laval drop-out, but it

was his own logic that kept pressing Lévesque further along the road
to independence. Logically and empirically, he did not believe that co-
operative federalism, however co-operative, could be 'a solution to
the problem of two nations.' 'Our "men of eminence," Pepin & Co ...
are really refusing to attack the problem of two nations. They believe
in empiricism and continuous extemporization in which the two-
nations contract will completely disappear. The fact is that ... our
"men of eminence" want permanent negotiation to replace all the
pledges and clauses whose purpose is to secure permanence for the
French-Canadian nation in a system where the minority forms the majority in only one government out of 11. Admittedly there is no such
thing as permanent security for any people, but the collective agreement is still essential.' Moreover, his experience in negotiating with
Ottawa, when he had become minister of welfare and demanded full
control over all aspects of social policy, confirmed his belief that Ottawa would never make the 'necessary adjustments.'

The Liberal defeat in 1966 at the hands of Daniel Johnson freed

Ottawa Citizen, November 30, 1967

Lévesque from the constraints of office and forced him, like other Liberals, to ponder the future orientation of the party. As the discussions among the Liberals went on, Lévesque left most of the others behind, such as Robert Bourassa, as he concluded that Pierre Trudeau was right – there was no middle ground. Political independence, combined if possible with an economic union with Canada, was the only logical answer to the tired question: What does Quebec want? In 1967 Lévesque declared that he wanted out of the century-old Canadian federation.

Others had reached the same conclusion years earlier.'If anyone had said to me twelve years ago, ''Around 1961 we'll have to take separatism seriously,'' I think I would just have shrugged it off,' André Laurendeau had written in the fall of 1961. By then there were three separatist groups in the province. The right-wing Alliance laurentienne, formed in 1957 by Raymond Barbeau, was the oldest. On the left was L'Action socialiste founded in August 1960 by Raoul Roy, publisher of *La Revue socialiste*. In September 1960 le Rassemblement

pour l'Indépendance national (RIN) appeared without a commitment to any social or economic order.

The RIN quickly became the most important, partly because of the activities of Dr Marcel Chaput in 1961. A Defence Research Board scientist in Ottawa, Dr Chaput resigned when he was suspended for attending a conference where he openly endorsed independence and returned to Montreal to a hero's welcome. 'Today the nation is ourselves, the revolution is ourselves; we are the national revolution,' cried Pierre Bourgault as the RIN hailed its first separatist martyr. By the end of 1961 a number of important Quebec organizations had endorsed the right to self-determination and *le Magazine Maclean* reported that 26.3 per cent of the three hundred Quebeckers interviewed by telephone supported independence and only 34.5 per cent were opposed.

Despite fierce internal battles over organization, ideology, and leadership, the RIN had become the leading separatist political party by 1966. Although other separatists could accept political sovereignty and a customs union with Canada, the left-wing ideology that had triumphed in the RIN had offended many. On the eve of the 1966 election the *Ralliement national* (RN) was created by the merger of several right-wing nationalist groups and advocated the establishment of an associate state within a Canadian common market. In the June election the RIN fielded seventy-three candidates and received 5.6 per cent of the popular vote, while the RN ran ninety candidates and received 3.2 per cent of the vote. However, the RIN received over 7 per cent in Montreal. Two hundred thousand Quebeckers voted for some form of independence, however ambiguous, and for parties that lacked leadership and organization.

René Lévesque was soon to provide some clarity and dynamic leadership, and his party the necessary organization.

1967

The Lévesque-Liberal separation

After a century of Confederation Canada needed 'a new pact, a new alliance between two nations,' claimed Daniel Johnson, Union nationale premier of Quebec. The first report of the Royal Commission on Bilingualism and Biculturalism warned that, however important the question of language, the basic Canadian problem was the 'degree of *self-determination* which one society can exercise in relation to another. To ignore the fundamental political dimensions of biculturalism,' wrote the commissioners, 'would not only constitute an error; it would very likely mean that Quebec would not listen to us.' But Quebec and the world listened to General Charles de Gaulle as he made his triumphant tour from Quebec to Montreal detecting and nourishing the feeling of liberation until on the balcony of the City Hall he uttered the fateful words, 'Vive le Québec libre!' The General's calculated indiscretion sharpened the debate, for not only did it seem to increase the credibility of the separatist option but the fury in the anglophone reaction persuaded many quasi-separatists to shed their last disguise. Alarmed at the growth of ultra-nationalism in Quebec, Prime Minister Pearson and his cabinet began the verbal reconquest of Quebec, while in Toronto Premier John Robarts summoned the provincial premiers to plan the Confederation for Tomorrow.

However, the really historical day was September 18, 1967, when René Lévesque spoke to his riding association in Montreal Laurier. For three hours the audience listened to his carefully structured and argued analysis of the past and present of French-English relations as

Toronto Star, July 22, 1967

he moved relentlessly towards his conclusion that independence, followed by some form of economic union, was the only solution. (The speech was published in *Le Devoir,* September 19-21.) The supporters then voted 37 to 7 for the following summary statement, which was to be presented at the October convention of the Quebec Liberal Federation:

'There are key moments in the existence of a nation when boldness and quiet courage become the only form of prudence that can be applied.

'If the nation does not then accept the calculated risk of major steps it can lose its destiny forever, exactly like a man who is afraid of life.

'Nevertheless, on the road to guaranteed survival and permanent progress on which no nation can be allowed to stop, we have been moving for some time towards a crucial crossroads. It is up to us to choose the political status which suits us best; that is to say, the road which permits us the most sure and efficient way to accomplish the necessary steps.

'On the one hand Quebec has attached itself in the last few years to an exhausting collective catching up in a large number of fields where backwardness had built up. As incomplete and imperfect as they are, these accomplishments have already allowed us to discover that the more we decide to undertake our "work" ourselves, the more we feel ourselves capable of succeeding as well as others.

'This very normal feeling of being better served by ourselves, added to the inevitable pressures of unceasingly increasing needs and aspirations, has resulted in the establishment of a more and more precise plan which is still expanding; the plan of rights that Quebec realizes it can not do without and the instruments and resources which it needs to exercise them. This ever-important plan, which no one has a right to ignore, constitutes for us a strict minimum.

'But on the other hand, it would seem that it would be dreaming to believe that for the rest of the country, this plan would not turn out to be a totally unacceptable maximum. From the viewpoint of a simple revision or even constitution revamping, what we would have to ask from all evidence surpasses not only the best of intentions shown in Ottawa and elsewhere but, without doubt, also the ability of the present federal regime to agree without fragmentation.

'If Quebec was to engage and persist in talks to revise the present structures, it is clear that in 100 years it still would not be out of the

woods. However, it is very probable that this nation which is now trying to make out of itself an acceptable homeland, would certainly not
want to speak of the past. This would periodically bring the lamenta-
ble return to the old defensive battles and skirmishes during which we
exhausted ourselves while neglecting the principle, as well as the falling back in electioneering at the two levels, harmful illusions of verbal
nationalism and, above all, the waste of energy that for us is surely the
most nefarious aspect of the regime.

'But this waste of energy is also felt on the English side of Canada.
The regime also hinders the other majority in its efforts to simplify, ra-
tionalize and centralize as it would like institutions which appear to it
as outdated.

'This is proof that it endures a sense of frustration which from all evidence is in danger of soon becoming intolerable.

'This parallel quest for two securities and two paths of collective
progress could not be continued in the present structures or anything
close to it, without our ending up with a double paralysis.

'Searching in the final analysis for the same thing – the chance to
live life in one's own way according to one's needs and priorities – the
two majorities would only continue to collide, always harder, one
against the other, always hurting each other, creating mutual harm
which would never end.

'We believe it is possible to avoid this joint dead-end by adapting to
our situations the two big currents that dominate our era: that of the
liberty of peoples and that of freely negotiated political and economi-
cal groups.

'Convinced among other things, that the danger is much less in a
clear and distinct option rather than in the present hesitations and increasing instability which accompanies it, we propose the following:

'First, we have to rid ourselves completely of the thoroughly-out-
dated federal regime. The problem can not resolve itself by the continuance or modification of the status quo.

'That means that we will have to dare claim for ourselves the entire
liberty of Quebec, its right to all the essential elements of independence, that is to say, the full control of each and every one of its principle collective decisions.

'That means that Quebec should become a sovereign state.

'Only in this way will we finally find security for our collective existence which otherwise would remain uncertain and crippled.

'Only in this way will we finally have the chance and obligation to exert to the maximum our energies and our talents to solve, without excuse or loophole, all important questions that concern us.

'In addition to being the only logical solution to the present Canadian impasse, it is also the sole common goal which can be overriding to the point of uniting us all, united strong enough to face all possible futures.

'To English Canada we must then propose to maintain an association not only of neighbors but also of partners in a common enterprise without which it would be, for one as well as the other, impossible to preserve and develop on this continent societies distinct from the United States.

'This undertaking would be made up essentially of the ties, of the complementary activities, of the innumerable economic inter-relationships within which we have learned to live. We would not destroy the framework in order to have, sooner or later, maybe too late, to rebuild it.

'Such an association seems to us tailored to permit us, without the encumbrance of constitutional rigidities, to make common cause with permanent consultations, flexible adjustments and appropriate mechanisms which our common economic interest requires: monetary union, a common tariff and co-ordination of fiscal policies. Nothing would prevent us – to the degree that we learn to understand each other better and to co-operate better in the context – from freely adding other areas where the same common action would seem mutually advantageous.

'In short, we would have a regime within which two nations, one whose homeland would be Quebec, the other arranging the rest of the country to suit itself, would associate themselves in a new adaptation of the current formula of the common markets to form a new entity which could, for example, call itself the "Canadian Union."'

'A poaching job,' commented Jean-Noël Tremblay, observing that 'I've been talking about it myself ever since 1962.' 'Another step towards the moment of truth,' wrote Claude Ryan (*Le Devoir,* September 20). One might regret that public men were incapable of containing their impatience, said Ryan, 'but the winds of freedom now blowing through Quebec are too insistent, it appears, to be calmed to the dictates of some coldly calculated timetable.' Reaffirming his own support for particular status within the federation (and arguing the case brilliantly on September 23), M. Ryan saw Lévesque's manifesto as forcing a clarification of positions and discussion: 'We are coming near the end of this time of ambiguities. The genuinely strong men of the era now beginning will be those who have been courageous enough to make clearcut choices and possess the force of intellect to uphold them.' Pierre Bourgault welcomed the new escalation and invited Lévesque and François Aquin to join the RIN. But the *Toronto Star*'s (September 20) warning against a too easy assumption that an economic union could be easily negotiated was repeated by most English-Canadians in the following weeks.

On September 23 and 24, when the young Liberals met at Stoneham, M.Lévesque met his first test. For thirty minutes he dazzled the group with his oratory and arguments: he hinted at new political alignments; discussed the psychological malaise in Quebec and Canada; played down the fears that an independent Quebec might become an authoritarian state; and repeated that there was no chance that English-Canada could ever accept the minimum demands of either the Liberals or the Union nationale. The game, he said, must end: 'They call it the Chinese torture ... We pull out a hair here, a feather there and after six months they say "let them have it, it will make them happy" ... and then fifteen days later it starts again.' But on September 24 the young Liberals voted 71 to 55 against independence. 'It was a screen test that demanded a choice that was too radical,' explained president Guy Morin. 'They were asked to say whether they were in favour of black or white when the reality is grey.' The critical decision awaited the October 15 conference.

The economic and political battle lines were drawn well before the conference opened. Politically, Eric Kierans and Jean Lesage forthrightly opposed independence, and the latter declared that he would not lead a separatist party. On October 1 at Sherbrooke Mr Kierans delivered a major attack on the economics of independence. Quebec, he argued, 'would not be a province like the others, it would be a lot poorer.' He estimated the loss over five years at $1.2 billion for the net loss of federal-financed services and $1.1 billion in declining revenues. Increased taxes, he said, would intensify the departure of corporations, curtail investment, and lead to an exodus of young talent. He challenged Finance Minister Dozois to deny that investment was falling off, asked why a prominent UN supporter had moved $800,000 to New York and Toronto in recent weeks, and argued that corporations such as Canadian Pacific, Canadian National, national life and trust companies, banks, Du Pont, CIL, Bell Telephone, and others would move their headquarters immediately. The thesis is simple, he told an enthusiastic audience which sang *O Canada* lustily: 'The separatism of Quebec would land Quebecers in misery, poverty and unemployment.'

Although Robert Bourassa, Liberal MLA and economic expert, refused to take sides, his detailed analysis made public on September 26 spelled out the economic dangers of independence: 'the devaluation of money, austerity measures, flight of capital, problems of borrowing in foreign markets and increases in the cost of imports.' To maintain the necessary rate of investment, he argued, the government of an independent Quebec would have to 'practise a policy which would hit the wage earners and benefit the profit margins of the investors.' He admitted that 'a judgment in economic terms cannot in itself either trigger independence movements or put a stop to them, but it should at least help ensure that the choice is not made in ignorance.' A poll of Liberal MLAs in late September showed that 88 per cent favoured a special status but opposed independence. The reasons were largely economic. 'People in my riding are not willing to sacrifice their standard of living or jeopardize their jobs' was a frequent comment.

M. Lévesque's defeat at the conference was predictable. Eric Kierans and the party organization had worked hard to make certain that M. Lévesque and separatism were eliminated root and branch, emphasizing the economic dangers of separatism and capitalizing on the opposition to Lévesque, the radical, among the party's old guard. As one group of delegates put it: 'We're not here to debate René Lévesque's arguments; what we're here to do is settle René Lévesque's hash.' The tone of the conference was indicated at once by the warm reception given Kierans and Lesage, as well as by the overwhelming defeat of the Lévesque group's attempt to secure a secret ballot.

On the afternoon of October 14, M. Paul Gérin-Lajoie introduced the official resolution from the Constitutional Affairs Committee:

'THE LIBERAL PARTY OF QUEBEC, based on the report by the Constitutional Affairs Committee submitted to the Convention of the Quebec Liberal Federation on 14 October 1967, affirms that: ...

'4. it believes nevertheless that a new Canadian constitution, including special status and increased powers for Quebec through a new division between the federal Parliament and that of Quebec, can best serve the political, economic, cultural, and social interests of the French Canadians;

'5. it thus rejects separatism in all its forms, for it would run counter to the higher interests of Quebec and the French-Canadian nation, would be achieved at the expense of the young, the workers, and the farmers, and could do injury to the policy of "Maîtres chez nous";

'6. it earnestly calls for a new Canadian constitution based on formal recognition of the presence of two nations in Canada and on the clearly demonstrated will to make French Canadians full members of a new Canadian confederation;

'7. the new constitution of Canada should, among other things, make provision for the establishment of a true constitutional court and for a declaration of the collective rights of minorities and majorities in Canada.'

Lévesque's speech supporting his 'independence – then negotiation' resolution was not among his best. Supporters of both positions were then allowed to make short statements, and among those opposing Lévesque were Lesage, Kierans, and Pierre Laporte. The burden of their argument was best summarized by M. Laporte when he declared: 'It is impossible for small nations to live otherwise than dangerously, but we do not in all conscience have the right to expose our people to the deadly risk of separatism, to escort them to utter disaster.' When the time came for his chance at rebuttal, René Lévesque declared that his proposal had not been seriously discussed, that the economic arguments against it ignored his view that a negotiated economic union was necessary, and that particular status was 'a dead-end without definition, a square peg in a round hole.' He charged that the organizers had wanted the conference to give 'a completely docile endorsement,' and warned that the Liberals were in danger once again of being a 'private club.' Then, following the strategy agreed upon in the early hours of the morning, he withdrew his resolution, announced his resignation from the party, and, joined by over one hundred supporters, walked out.

But the ghost remained to be laid, and the Lévesque resolution was kept on the floor. Towards midnight the vote was taken. Only nine (Le Devoir counted four) hands were raised in favour of his proposal, and there were twelve declared abstentions. Twelve opposed the official resolution, and there were ten abstentions. And, as Paul Cliche (Le Devoir, October 16) bitterly wrote, a delegate asked that the session close with the singing of O Canada: 'Mr Kierans complied proudly. And it was the final measures of O Canada that launched the Liberal Party of Quebec on the way to its new destiny.'

That destiny was far from certain, for the convention did not debate the detailed report from the constitutional committee spelling out the details of particular status. The highly controversial document (published in *La Presse,* October 12) was described by Eric Kierans before the conference as a working document, whereas its author, Paul Gérin-Lajoie, regarded it as the basis of the general resolution placed before the conference. The issue was avoided when Pierre Laporte referred it to the political committee for study before being submitted to a special convention in 1968. The 72-clause report called for widespread new powers for Quebec: radio and television; increased powers on immigration; complete control over social security and manpower; direct participation in the formation of monetary and tariff policy; marriage and divorce; commercial and financial corporations; full power in international affairs for all matters within its jurisdiction; possibly control over such matters as fisheries and some forms of transport; and the necessary financial powers to reflect the legislative responsibilities. Federally, the report called for radical changes in the Senate and the Supreme Court, a bill of rights guaranteeing minority rights, and asked whether the country should not be a republic. Provincially, it called for the abolition of the monarchy, the end of appeals to courts outside the province, and a bill of rights. Unless such a status was secured immediately, concluded the report, 'there is a risk of a rapid deterioration in the situation, with the potential for a rupture.'

The report, said M. Lesage, was federalist, for it did not do away with the federal Parliament. But the *Globe and Mail* (October 12) replied that 'by any other name, separatism [is] still separatism,' while Ben Malkin (*Ottawa Citizen,* October 12) declared that 'no matter how thin you slice it, that's *separatism.'* Maurice Western (*Winnipeg Free Press,* October 13) commented that, if adopted, 'the country, having been saved from separatism, would simply fly apart.' In an open telegram to M. Gérin-Lajoie, Dean Maxwell Cohen wrote: 'It is without doubt a document that would be totally unacceptable to anyone who believes in a united Canada. While it is a serious approach it is essentially a republican semi-separatist approach and its conception of Canadian federalism is one which would destroy the Canada we know, and therefore it should be totally unacceptable to any responsible Quebec political party.' But on the eve of the conference that staunch supporter of the federalist option, Claude Ryan, commenting on such English-Oanadian attitudes, had observed: 'Some elements in English Canada have but one obsession: they want Quebec to produce an anti-separatist profession of faith. The rest is so much Greek and rubbish to them. The Quebec Liberals should not play into the hands of this narrow group. Certainly, if such is their conviction, they should openly reject separatism. But beyond this rejection, their best efforts should be directed at defining, courageously and precisely, what Quebec wants, what Quebec desires. Now the basic aspirations of the Quebec of 1967 strike me as being closer to M. Gérin-Lajoie's concerns than to anti-separatism.' M. Ryan felt that, in the short term at least, Lévesque had badly misjudged Quebec opinion. But at a press conference after his resignation M. Lévesque declared that the separatists could win power in four years. An election in 1967, he said on October 30, would give the separatists from 25 to 30 per cent of the vote. For the remainder of the year he toured Quebec and Canada, pressing the logic for his case to English and French alike. It was inevitable that René Lévesque would emerge as the leader of a political movement, and as early as November 11 he held discussions with Pierre Bourgault, leader of the RIN. Finally, on the weekend of November 18 and 19 (when both the Liberal and UN parties held private meetings to ponder the state of 'the nation'), over three hundred people from all parts of Quebec with a 'mutual interest' in his proposals met with M. Lévesque in Montreal. By the end of the weekend the Mouvement Souveraineté-Association had appeared. The aim was to form a new political party which would 'regroup' all elements which supported the independence of Quebec. Meanwhile, a series of regional meetings were planned, and the executive was empowered to undertake negotiations with other separatist parties. The first meeting of the mouvement, held at Sept-Iles on December 9, netted one additional MLA when François Aquin was on the platform with M. Lévesque and announced his adhesion: 'There is only one man who can assume the leadership of the party that will achieve independence,' he exclaimed. 'That man is René Lévesque.' The latter in turn declared: 'Five years from now, at the outside, will see the election of a Québécois party with a clear mandate from the people to negotiate independence and economic association. Within that time English Canadians will have seen a majority form in Quebec. We must prepare ourselves for independence, and so develop the climate for it.'

Three days later Pierre Bourgault, back from his supposedly successful fund-raising trip to Paris, told 1,500 enthusiastic supporters that RIN would make every effort to unite with the mouvement (attending the meeting were M. Aquin and Jean-Marc Léger, the *Le Devoir* journalist who in three lengthy articles late in October opted finally for independence and left the editorial page). A day later Bourgault added at Collégé Sainte-Marie that he would gladly yield the leadership of the separatist movement to M. Lévesque. On December 12, too, RN Leader Gilles Grégoire told Laval students that the differences between separatists were much less than their common bond, and that all would rally together to achieve their end. Perhaps the most surprising turn of events came on December 18, when Marcel Pépin, leader of the Confederation of National Trade Unions (CNTU), and Louis Laberge of the Quebec Labour Federation announced that they had asked M. Lévesque for a meeting to discuss his proposals. Observers speculated that the labour leaders were concerned about M. Lévesque's impact on the rank and file as suggested by the heavy turnout of trade unionists at some of his meetings. Pépin and Laberge declared that they intended to meet with others who had 'precise constitutional positions' as well, but gave no names.

Any union of the forces for independence was made difficult not only by Lévesque's insistence that he was not a separatist, but also by sharp differences of opinion about internal policy for the new nation. The difficulty could be seen both in attempts to bring the RN and RIN together, which led to the selection of Marcel Chaput as a mediator by the RN late in May, and in problems within the RIN itself, which came into the open at the RIN convention at Three Rivers on October 7 to 8. While one issue was the determination of Pierre Bourgault to quell what he described as anarchistic tendencies within the party (or what his opponents charged was his determination to establish 'a cult of personality'), the major questions concerned the related questions of ideology and some fusion with the right-wing RN. At the convention Bourgault asked for increased executive control and 'conditional fusion' with the RN, while the left-wing, led by Mme André Bertrand-Ferreti, opposed any deal with the RN and insisted that the RIN be a party of the working class. Bourgault was re-elected, but his opponents won many of the positions on the executive. The crisis over the RN-RIN fusion, which could have shattered the party, was resolved by a motion from five members of the Front de Libération du Québec (FLQ) who asked for ten minutes in return for the years spent in jail. They persuaded the meeting to approve a study of 'all possibilities for closer relations with independentist individuals and groups, with a view to their joining the RIN.'

1968

The Parti québécois emerges

1968 would be the 'year of decision,' said Prime Minister Pearson as he launched the first of the constitutional conferences that was to undertake a total review of Canadian federalism. The architect of the federal position was Pierre Trudeau, elected Liberal leader in April and confirmed by the electorate as prime minister in the June 25 election. Long recognized as a federalist and a champion of French-Canadian language and culture, Mr Trudeau was also blunt in his condemnation of ultra-nationalism whether it took the form of two nations, special status, associate state, or independence. Federal policy rejected the claim for special status, and was built upon the assumption that if linguistic and cultural equality for francophones could be guaranteed on the national level Quebec could be treated as a province like the others: nationalism and federalism could be treated as separate questions. But in Quebec nationalism burst out in the streets of Montreal on June 24, St Jean Baptiste day, as the prime minister was attacked by a mob of students led by Pierre Bourgault and the RIN. And the long-simmering question of the language of education for immigrant children boiled over in St Leonard.

The separatist movement became a more important political force in Quebec than ever before, as René Lévesque's Mouvement Souveraineté-Association became a political party and absorbed both the RIN and the RN. The year opened with the publication of Lévesque's *Option Québec* on January 17, which immediately became a best seller. On March 30, after a bitter struggle between Pierre Bourgault and

Mme André Bertrand-Ferreti, the RIN voted to form a common front with the MSA. At an April 20-21 convention the MSA decided to become a full-fledged political party within six months. While Lévesque's call for unity received a rousing reception, only his forceful statement that he had no desire to be a member of a racist party prevented the convention from adopting a resolution in favour of unilingualism.

The events of June 24 in Montreal, when Bourgault was arrested, made more difficult any merger of the MSA with the RIN, but on August 2, the MSA and RN agreed to unite. Three days later the joint executive committees issued a statement of objectives which included the creation of a French-language sovereign state; the establishment of a democracy 'that will not be merely electoral, but economic, social and cultural,' and 'where the fundamental rights of the individual and of recognized minority groups will be respected equally scrupulously, including the school-rights of the English-speaking minority'; and the negotiation of a treaty with Canada for an economic association in the form of a tariff and monetary community.

The Parti québécois was born in Quebec City at an October 11–14 convention. M. Lévesque's opening address was less a call for independence, than a cry for a new society, a form of participatory democracy that would lead to a revolt against all outdated and rigid social, economic, and political structures. Participation was the key word at the convention as delegates debated hundreds of amendments submitted by riding associations to the draft program drawn up in April. A program far more radical than that advocated by the leaders was finally adopted. On the sensitive subject of minority language and educational rights the convention agreed to the continuance of English-language schools on a limited basis, but declared that immigrants would be required to speak French and attend French-language schools, that English would not be an official language, and that businesses would have five years to convert to French. While foreign investment was to be permitted, corporations would have to hire a majority of their executives in Quebec and re-invest a portion of their profits. The independence of Quebec was not to be negotiated, and discussions with Canada would follow the unilateral declaration of independence. Universal medicare, the nationalization of land on the perimeter of cities, state planning, the creation of a Bank of Quebec were all approved; but, after lengthy debate, a resolution proposing centralization and secularization of the universities and the government of educational institutions by students and professors was narrowly defeated. On the final day the convention adopted the title, Parti québécois, and Lévesque predicted that it would hold the balance of power after the next provincial election. The press seemed impressed with the session. The *Montreal Star* (December 15) spoke of the realism, idealism, moderation, and reasoned discussion and warned English Canada not to regard the PQ 'as just another pack of frustrated, embittered extremists.'

Ten days later the union of the separatist groups was complete as the convention of the RIN voted overwhelmingly for dissolution and union with the PQ. When the vote was announced Bourgault declared: 'For the last time in my life, I say "Long live the RIN!" And for the first time in my life, I say "Long live the Parti québécois!" ' While a Gallup Poll released on October 16 revealed that only 11 per cent of Quebeckers supported separatism, with 17 per cent undecided (compared to 13 and 10 in Ontario!), the PQ had an estimated 25,000 members, and embryonic organizations in most provincial constituencies. Separatism had undoubtedly become a major political force in Quebec and Canada.

COMBATTRE POUR SON PAYS

Toronto Star, February 7, 1968

1969

Organizing for the 'great adventure'

In Ottawa the Trudeau government passed the Official Languages Act, while in Quebec the pressure mounted for a more unilingual society. As the prime minister sought to separate nationalism and federalism, Premier Johnson entered round two of the constitutional conference with the proposition that Canada become an economic union of two semi-sovereign states and an association of two equal nations. Terror reigned in Montreal as bombs rocked public buildings, and vandalism and violence, robbery, arson, and murder walked the streets. The provincial government outlined a ten-point programme to combat the terrorists, and on October 7 asked Ottawa to send troops to Montreal when a police strike was the occasion for a regime of lawlessness promoted in part by radical nationalists and terrorists. In Ottawa the Prime Minister painted a gloomy picture of life in an independent Quebec: 'The worm is already in the bud,' he warned, but fortunately 'Separatism is still, I say it again, an obscure and minor party no member of which has been or will be elected. The mere thought that it could happen is enough to make Quebec turn backward.'

One of the most outspoken opponents of terror and violence in Quebec was René Lévesque, leader of the Parti québécois, popularly known as the PQ or les Péquistes. Yet the PQ had by far the most to gain from the economic uncertainty, the social malaise, and the lack of political leadership in the province. Not only was M. Lévesque the most dynamic and talented political leader in Quebec, but he and his party appealed to far more than the desire for independence. As revealed in lengthy interviews with the leaders of the three parties published in *La Presse* and the *Montreal Star* (January 9), Lévesque alone captured the substance and the vocabulary of the age of contestation: 'one is led to wonder whether modern industrial societies by inflating their bureaucracies and dividing their people between narrower and ever tighter social and professional classes, have not in the end weakened social sense or the feeling of belonging. They may even have lessened men's feeling of happiness in inverse ratio to the rise of living standards.' His radical image and appeal to youth was ideally suited to a society where thousands of students, newly enfranchised, were heading from the schools and the CEGEPS into a society that had little place for them, and where the working class was suffering from high unemployment (see, for example, Michel Roy's report on a Toronto *Telegram-Le Devoir* survey in *Le Devoir,* July 17).

Every survey of Quebec opinion during the year showed the PQ increasing in popular support. In the *Toronto Star* (April 26) that indefatigable head-counter Peter Regenstreif reported that 26 per cent of French-speaking Canadians supported the PQ, while 41 per cent believed that independence was inevitable. Two months later (June 28) the *Telegram* survey concluded that 26 per cent of the Quebec population favoured independence, and that among those twenty-five and under the figure soared to 43 per cent. M. Lévesque's frequent appearances on television, his incessant public speeches and organizational tours of the province, and his diligent ambulance-chasing of labour problems and educational crises undoubtedly accounted for his rising popularity. Political action committees among trade unionists, the teachers unions, and students' organizations enabled the PQ to infiltrate and secure new adherents. Teachers and priests, in particular, seemed to be joining the students to swell the ranks of les péquistes.

The credibility of the PQ was increased dramatically on September 19 when Jacques Parizeau announced that he would run as a PQ candidate in the next election. A well-known economist, who had served as adviser to both the Liberals and the Union nationale, Professor Parizeau declared that Quebec was already 'half torn' from Canada and, since it could not be reattached, 'the tearing process must be carried through to the end.' Whatever its merits, Mr. Parizeau's explanation, as he gave it to the *Toronto Star* (November 12), provided an interesting commentary on the evolution of Canadian federalism between 1957 and 1969:

'The Canadian federation had in fact followed a path quite unique in the modern world. As other federations tended to become much more centralized, we had followed the opposite path, divesting the central government of huge resources, the allocation of which was either totally unconditional or shortly to be so. The government function and the government processes had been divided up. Pitched battles not only with respect to the division of powers but to their use sterilized action or reduced it to a very slow pace indeed.

'While public opinion and the press were calling for imaginative policies and politicians were announcing all manners of new deals and just societies, in fact the government process was bogged down in more than 150 federal-provincial committees. A Just Society? By all means, so long as one recognized that unemployment insurance belongs to one government, and unemployment assistance to another; old-age security to the first, public pension plan to the other; one makes money available for housing, the other has the right of initiative for all projects. What does one then promise: half a just society or a half just society?

'Schemes pertaining to special status for Quebec or associate statehood thus only appeared to be devices to increase the disorder and the inefficiency of government. Indeed there is more at stake in such disorganization than constitutional battles. Bad or slow performance by government had a price in our days. And while we may all relish our high standard of living, this is becoming a myth. The rate of growth of the Canadian economy has not been all that impressive in relation to others, and the performance in eastern Canada has been poor. To tell a French Canadian living in Quebec or an average wage earner in New Brunswick that he has the second highest standard of living in the world is a fraud.

'However, thanks to the integration of the Canadian economy with that of the u.s., the dismantling of our government has not had the very serious effects that it could have had otherwise.

'But the time has come to rebuild the government. And there is really only one way to do it – that is, to recentralize Canada. Not only to stop balkanization at the point it has reached, but to backtrack. In that light I fully understand the attitude of those, either French or English Canadians, who wish to locate the government, the real government, in Ottawa. It is a coherent, logical and historically respectable position.

'I feel, nevertheless, that by and large most French Canadians will never accept that solution. Traditionally they have been quite satisfied to play both ends against the middle. A number of them still are ready, in the words of a federal minister, "to be separatists against Trudeau and federalists against Lévesque." If, however, they must choose unequivocally – as I think they now must, and probably as events will force them to do anyhow – it is simply impossible for me to see how they will choose the Ottawa solution.

'Thus if it is not possible to rebuild a proper government in Ottawa, only one path is still opened: to build one in Quebec City.'

With the threat of economic disaster the leading anti-separatist argument, Lévesque hailed Parizeau's decision as a major breakthrough. It would, he exclaimed, 'dissipate artificial fears ... in the domain of economics, fears which some people are paid to encourage.'

Professor Parizeau was second only to M. Lévesque at the party's convention in Montreal's sports arena, October 17 to 19. Delegates to the convention numbered 1,015, of whom 22 per cent were teachers, 18 per cent students, 11 per cent civil servants, 2 per cent farmers, and 9 per cent members of the working class. Two-thirds of the delegates were under thirty-five. Lévesque determined the goal and set the tone of the convention in his opening address, asking the delegates to avoid the 'impulsive high-mindedness' and 'spectacular about-faces' of the past. Already, he said, 'our platform has given us ... the look of a party that may very possibly, and perhaps very soon, be forming a government. This is what we've wanted; let's not spoil our success with amateurish enthusiasm.' The entire convention was marked by order and moderation – 'controlled passion,' Michel Roy called it – and the delegates accepted Lévesque's discreet encouragement not to elect Pierre Bourgault to the executive committee and voted instead for Parizeau, Marc-André Bédard (financier), Claude Charron (student), and Dr Camille Laurin (psychiatrist).

Resolutions provided for an independent Quebec to become a modified parliamentary republic, with the National Assembly composed in part of elected representatives and in part of additional members selected according to the popular vote of each party. The state's army was to be transformed into a peace corps. The most significant resolutions dealt with the economy. Led by Parizeau the convention approved proposals for an openly state-controlled economy, but with room for private investment including foreign investment: 'As for firms with foreign capital Quebec will continue to welcome them and they will be treated with respect provided they behave as good citizens.

'The state (1) will participate, when necessary and opportune, in their investments; (2) will establish rules for their relations with their head office; (3) will make sure they hire a majority of Quebeckers in their executive staff and, if needed, will give them a precise period of grace to train them.'

The economic resolutions also included ownership restrictions on banks and insurance companies, established a farmers' commission to control imports of farm products, and provided for the decertification of Canadian and international unions to permit only Quebec unions. On the controversial schools question, the convention rejected Raymond Lemieux's appeal for unilingual schools in favour of the continued existence of English-language schools. René Lévesque amplified his views on this and other matters at an informal press conference on October 18 when he declared that his party would win ten seats and 20 per cent of the vote at the next election.

'M. Lévesque then went on the attack against a "wealthy, influential" English-speaking Montreal minority "who don't want to let go of their privileges and prerogatives." The PQ leader accused this English minority of raising spectres, spreading delusions, and engaging in "mental terrorism" by systematically labelling as "separatist" everything under the headings of violence, activism, terrorism, etc. M. Lévesque worried also about an approach he sees as increasingly evident among newspaper editors, which aggravates the public disorders and even comes close to provoking them by a sensational treatment of the various acts of violence that vitiate the current atmosphere. "But what will happen to a Quebec Anglophone when Quebec reaches independence?" someone asked. "Nothing," was M. Lévesque's answer, "except that he will have to speak French. I won't be the one to tell the English-speaking people how many minutes they should spend studying French in school; I won't tell them to do 50 or 55 minutes of French a day, but I will insist that they speak French." M. Lévesque went on to add that his government would issue no diploma, no licence to carry on a profession or trade, not even a driving licence, unless the applicant had done an examination certifying his knowledge of French. "They'll go to Berlitz or elsewhere, they'll organize, they'll work things out any way they please – that's not my problem," he said; "all that will be required of them is that they speak French."

'The PQ chief lashed out violently against "those tiny groups representing nobody that call themselves Maoist, Guevarist, or whatever ...

I can understand the sentimentalism that affects some young people
somewhat like a drug, but can I, in all decency – simply to gain the ad-
miration, the adoration of a handful of sensation-crazed little terrorists
– keep spewing out tough denunciations of everything that exists,
everything that is?'' On the other hand, M. Lévesque said the current
atmosphere, with its demonstrations as well as its acts of terrorism,
put his party in a fairly uncomfortable or at least embarrassing position: "It's annoying having to issue constant statements dissociating
ourselves from such or such a thing done by such or such a
movement." He pointed out, however, that activism benefits the Parti
québécois by increasing people's political awareness and focusing
attention on "the stagnation of our present situation." Indirectly too,
the disorders serve his party's cause by considerably weakening existing power groups, in particular the Union nationale: "Never have I
seen a party fall apart as quickly and dramatically as the Union nationale is now doing." Returning to the acts of violence and those who
commit them (he cited the Company of Young Canadians), M. Lévesque said he was refusing to play into the hands "of those few lumi-
naries who are using the Montreal taxi drivers they couldn't care less
about to get them to their own objective – the mindless overthrow of
existing authority, whatever its label."

   'M. Lévesque, in fact, saw no reason why there should not be excellent relations between independent Quebec and Ottawa. Moreover,
he feels Canada will have to be conciliatory and will have nothing to
gain by burning its bridges. "You only have to glance at the map," he
insisted. M. Lévesque envisaged Quebec between Canada of the Maritimes and Canada of the West just as Canada itself lies between the
United States and their state of Alaska. Questioned about the various
types of agreements that might be reached on different subjects, the
PQ leader admitted that the situation has yet to be examined in complete detail, and that it would be the specific objective of Quebec-Ottawa negotiations to find agreement in all these areas. He did foresee,
however, the establishment of a Quebec railway corporation, a national or mixed airline company, and so on, though all this would be
done without closing the doors and severing the ties, without
"shutting ourselves up behind a sort of Chinese wall." The party is
known to be planning to build teams of negotiators whose role will be
to reach, with Ottawa, the constitutional terms and policies by which
the sovereign country of Quebec will still remain an ally of the rest of
Canada.' (*Le Devoir*, October 20)

For the remainder of the year Lévesque, Parizeau, and company continued the work of organization and publicity. M. Lévesque's chief goal appeared to be to remove the fear of independence, suggesting it was deliberately fostered by the enemies of separatism and arguing that all that had to be feared was fear itself. At any rate, why deny ourselves this 'great adventure'? At their March 6 to 9 assembly in Montreal the Estates General had adopted a totally separatist position, and in November 15 to 16 the Quebec Federation of St Jean Baptiste Societies declared 117 to 16 for independence, the Quebec City, Sherbrooke, Valleyfield, and St Jérôme chapters opting out. This probably did not represent any new strengths, however, for both decisions had been predictable for several years.

1970

Strike one: the election of April 29

In Ottawa the premiers continued their constitutional discussions, while a terrorist bomb killed a francophone woman and injured two soldiers. In Quebec, where the Liberals chose Robert Bourassa as their leader and the voters returned a Liberal government in the April 29 election, there was no let-up in terrorist activities. Two of the leaders, Charles Gagnon and Pierre Vallières, free on bail, openly campaigned for better revolutionary organization and activity. Evidence mounted that the radicals had a cache of arms, and that the FLQ planned to kidnap a hostage to be used for political purposes. Finally on October 5 with the kidnapping of James Cross and the later kidnapping and murder of Pierre Laporte, the country faced the worst and most tragic domestic crisis in its history. René Lévesque was unable to escape some involvement in the October crisis. Writing in *Le Journal de Montréal* on October 8 he dissociated the Parti québécois from the FLQ and denounced the 'sewer rats' who resorted to kidnapping. But 'the blind brutality of bureaucracies, technologies, and so-called "growth" economies appear more important than human beings,' he added, and 'the all too frequent and visible collusion between private exploitation and public administration' provided an understandable explanation for terrorism. Throughout the crisis he advocated a negotiated settlement and was among the most outspoken in his criticism of the use of the army and the War Measures Act.

Towards April 29

Seldom, if ever, has a Quebec election been watched more closely by the English-Canadian media. Yet the general ignorance or indifference of much of the population may well offer its own comment on the likely success of the political and constitutional accommodation to nationalism and biculturalism. For in a year that was to see the dramatic events of October, a Gallup Poll published on April 18 revealed that 39 per cent of Canadians could not say who they wanted to win in Quebec. Political allegiances die hard in the Maritimes and the west, where 18 and 16 per cent respectively opted for a Conservative victory although the Conservative party had not fought in a provincial election in Quebec since 1935. Only one thing was certain: virtually no one outside Quebec was a supporter of René Lévesque.

In retrospect, Jean-Jacques Bertrand's decision on March 12 to have a snap dissolution and an April 29 election seemed like a gross miscalculation. Yet if the Union nationale still suffered from ambiguities on policy and personal rivalries not yet stilled from its 1969 leadership convention, the party at least had its équipe, its patronage, and its finance. On the other hand, the Liberals had a new and untried leader and M. Bourassa's scars of victory were still raw; the Ralliement créditiste, always a possible threat to the rural-based Union nationale, had a leadership convention before it; and René Lévesque's Péquistes were far from ready for an election. With a strike-promised summer, the decision seemed sound. And within a few days an election platform, promising everything but lower taxes, was ready for the electorate.

The Bourassa Liberals were far readier than M. Bertrand imagined. The organization that had won the convention had retained its momentum. Within days of the announcement of the election the Liberals received the results of a small poll of thirty constituencies and five hundred voters, which gave the Liberals 18 per cent, the Parti québécois 14.3 per cent, the Union nationale 12.6, the Créditistes 9.3, and left 42.6 undecided. Not only did the Liberals accept the validity of the poll and conclude that Lévesque was their major enemy, but they also accepted the poll's insight into the issues that disturbed the electorate: unemployment, 47.8 per cent; education, 17.5 per cent; the economy, 10 per cent; high taxes, 9.6 per cent; industrialization, 9.3 per cent; the high cost of living, 6.3 per cent. Well behind these interrelated issues were questions of language, separatism, and provincial autonomy which concerned only 3, 1.5, and .5 per cent of the population respectively. 'QUEBEC TO WORK!' became the slogan and '100,000 new jobs in 1971!' the promise; the means a Liberal team of competent administrators headed by the cool and confident technocrat running a Quebec that remained resolutely within 'a profitable federalism.' As M. Bourassa hammered home the Liberal theme, Liberal organizers built up a formidable organization and blanketed the province with carefully planned radio and television programmes and flying visits from M. Bourassa. By February 16 Paul Desrochers predicted victory in 72 seats, and on the eve of the election Liberal organizers claimed to be certain of 62 and named a dozen others where the odds favoured the party.

René Lévesque's appeal was as direct in its essentials as M. Bourassa's. Across from the large ads 'QUEBEC: TO WORK' was a picture of M. Lévesque urging the electorate to vote 'YES.' 'We are – Québécois' read the lettering on the blackboard, while bold type declared:

'THE TIME HAS COME TO SAY: YES

YES, to normal liberty in friendship with others.

YES, to normal security, and an end to prying.

YES, to normal responsiblility, which is the only true driving force for progress at every level, beginning with the economy.

YES, quite simply to a normal life in a normal Quebec.

YES, on April 29, let's vote for Quebec.'

Lévesque appealed to the young, the left, and the discontented, to those tired of the old parties and the wasted energy of decades of conflict with Ottawa. Although his programme was starkly nationalist, his tone was not shrill as he urged the Québécois not to believe that the economic price of independence was high and pleaded with them to withdraw their old fears and their subservient attitude towards English Canada and the local establishment. On the controversial language issue he promised both to make French the only official language and to respect the educational rights of the minority.

Just as Bourassa had selected the Péquistes as his prime target, so did Lévesque spend most of his time attacking the Liberals. He was concerned too that the Créditistes, under their new provincial leader Camille Samson, would pick up discontented votes in the rural areas from the flagging Union nationale which might otherwise have gone Parti québécois. By April 26 he was charging that the Créditistes were being manipulated by the Liberal machine – others suggested that the Liberals were not sorry to see the Créditistes in the field – and urged them to join the Parti québécois and help 'clean house.'

M. Samson, meanwhile, was running a predictable campaign, appealing to rural discontent, applying conventional Social Credit solutions to the problems of poverty and unemployment, and arguing that the federal system was workable provided Quebec had control over credit and all matters within its jurisdiction, including direct taxation and social welfare.

As the three opposition parties – the provincial NDP was never a factor even in the eleven Montreal seats where it ran candidates – maintained a furious momentum, the Union nationale appeared to stagger and then collapse. The party began the election without a coherent platform, and remained throughout on the defensive. Prime Minister Bertrand's promise on April 5 that the UN would hold a referendum on independence by 1974 unless a new constitution had been drafted (apparently at the urging of Finance Minister Mario Beaulieu) seemed to be a futile attempt to find middle ground between Bourassa's federalism and Lévesque's independence. Without satisfying the more nationalistic members of the Union nationale it may even have forced UN members into the Liberal, PQ, or Créditiste camps. The UN position was further weakened when Marcel Masse, speaking to students at Ste Foy on April 22, declared that the only difference between the Union nationale and the Parti québécois was that of immediate independence or waiting on events until 1974. Reprimanded by Bertrand, M. Masse then even suggested the possibility of a UN-PQ coalition if the government found itself in a minority.

Long before the election the Union nationale appeared to be 'running scared.' The promises became more generous – more unlikely of fulfilment too as M. Beaulieu forecast a billion dollar deficit at an April 10 press conference – and the attack on Ottawa's miserliness more strident. A *La Presse* poll, published on April 18, revealed that the Union nationale had fallen to third place with only 13.4 per cent of the votes. A *Montreal Star* poll of a few constituencies, published on April 25, also showed the UN trailing the Liberals and the Péquistes, as did a Peter Regenstreif poll published in the *Toronto Star* (April 24) which gave the Liberals 32 per cent, the PQ 23, the UN 16, and the Créditistes 9. The polls enabled the Union nationale to charge that the press was against them, while M. Bertrand gamely replied that he was out to win elections, not polls. But the polls and the opposition of most newspapers to the UN provided the opportunity to lash out in a last desperate attack on his enemies. On April 26, while Justice Minister Rémi Paul was asserting that while not all Péquistes were terrorists all terrorists were members of the Parti québécois and that Lévesque was the Castro of Quebec, M. Bertrand was picturing the election as a giant plot of the financiers to destroy him. In a speech apparently only partly delivered because his audience sat on their hands, he linked the newspaper polls with the financial interests of Montreal and Toronto. The *Montreal Star* and the *Gazette* might be expected to support the Liberals but he took special pains to point out that *La Presse* was owned by the Power Corporation, and rang all the changes on the links between the Power Corporation and the Liberal party from Peter Nesbitt Thomson (first vice-chairman of the board) to Marc Lalonde and M. Bourassa's brothers-in-law. 'Don't we have the right to ask questions in the face of the tentacles we see that link all these men to the Liberal party, provincially and federally?' But in the last few days he seemed to move away from that bravado to urge traditional UN supporters not to be complacent and to ask for a law and order mandate to stamp out radicals and terrorists.

The issues of French-English and federal-provincial relations could hardly be kept out of the campaign. M. Bourassa did his best to minimize them, refusing to be drawn into constitutional discussions about

Toronto Star, April 23, 1970

'profitable federalism' and arguing that while 'French must be the working language of Quebec, we don't have to break up Canada to achieve that goal.' But both Beaulieu and Lévesque kept hammering away at the old tax game, picturing a virtuous Quebec as the innocent victim of federal rape. M. Beaulieu continually drew attention to the $200 million that Quebec claimed from taxes levied to finance medicare, and on April 23 published in *Le Devoir* a letter to Finance Minister Edgar Benson in which he wondered why justice was not done to Quebec when the wheat farmers collected $100 million, Nova Scotia $40 million, and recipients of foreign aid the $200 million recommended by Lester Pearson.

Throughout this attack both M. Bourassa and the federal Liberals remained quiet. But on April 23 the Quebec wing of the Liberal party of Canada published its 250,000-circulation monthly bulletin, *Quoi de Neuf*. The bulletin provided a detailed breakdown of all figures and concluded that in 1968-69 Quebec gained $547 million. The bulletin added that the federal government employed more than ninety thousand Québécois, purchased $357 million worth of goods in Quebec, and would invest more than $400 million in Quebec during the fiscal year. The annual net gain, claimed *Quoi de Neuf*, was more than one billion dollars. The editors claimed to be reluctant to enter the controversy, but wrote that 'For several years ... the federal government has refused to engage in this sterile discussion which seeks to measure the advantages of federalism in auditing terms. It is nonetheless true that these provincial politicians who try to make us believe that we are being toyed with by Ottawa, with the aid of figures which they carefully avoid explaining because they can't do it, have spread fears which must be dissipated.' Questioned in Ottawa, Secretary of State Gérard Pelletier shrugged off the suggestion that this was federal intervention: 'I think it has always been understood amongst us that when Confederation is threatened, we could not stand idly by ... We would reply with facts and figures and answers. That is what we have done' (*Ottawa Citizen*, April 24). Bertrand and Lévesque immediately hailed the document as proving their charges that Bourassa was a puppet of Ottawa. M. Bourassa himself denounced the document as a 'propaganda bulletin' which contained debatable figures and its publication as 'badly timed, awkward, and without justification.' Not for the first or last time, Prime Minister Trudeau was forced to undercut one of his Quebec ministers. On April 26 his office issued a press release stating that M. Bertrand's accusation of federal intervention was an 'accusation without foundation.' The bulletin was published by the party 'without prior approval or censorship of the federal government in general and of its prime minister in particular as is normal in a truly democratic party.' Ottawa had not intervened, the statement concluded, 'and in spite of the provocation of certain provincial politicians, it does not intend to do so.'

Although the Bourassa Liberals were aware of the danger that could come from Ottawa's intervention, there were many English Canadians who waited for the Trudeau team to swing into action. Alarmed by the apparent strength of Lévesque, the *Globe and Mail* wondered editorially on April 21 whether the time had not come for Mr Trudeau to enter the campaign:

'It is tradition to assume that Quebec resents any Ottawa intervention in its provincial elections, but this is not a provincial election like any other provincial election. The fate of the country could be riding upon it.

'Mr. Trudeau and his Quebec colleagues have a duty to present to their constituents the federal side of the issue and point out the folly of electing a party committed to breaking up the country.

'They have plenty of ammunition to use, for a separated Quebec would be an impoverished and unhappy place, and Mr. Lévesque, as La Presse has pointed out, has left all of the hard facts out of his pretty picture of sovereignty. Mr. Trudeau is also the only man with an emotional currency in Quebec to match that of Mr. Lévesque. He cannot leave the field to him until after April 29.' Some observers felt that position was shared by many MPs.

Within Quebec the English-Canadian minority worked valiantly to secure M. Bourassa's victory. On April 3 the Montreal investment firm of Lafferty and Hardwood advised its clients to ship their securities and liquid assets outside the province until after the election. The Montreal dailies left no doubt of their position. And on April 26 the Royal Trust openly sent a shipload of securities out of the province in nine Brinks trucks. Whether these ploys led the timid to vote Liberal rather than PQ or UN could not be determined, but they certainly fanned the flames of separatist anger and undoubtedly did little to ease English-French relations within the province.

On the eve of the election the Montreal press attempted to provide its readers with an overview of the campaign. The *Gazette*, editorially committed to the Liberals, provided a comparative chart of the parties' platforms on key issues; it is reproduced on pages 38-41.

In his relentlessly thorough way Claude Ryan surveyed the scene and made his choice in long editorials (*Le Devoir*, April 23-25). Confessing that no one could predict the results he wrote:

'The people of Quebec must first decide whether they will vote to break the federal link with the rest of Canada or to retain this link during the next four years. They may have a thousand different reasons for supporting the Parti québécois. They should not forget that, in voting for this party, they are voting in favour of Quebec's political separation from the rest of Canada.

'As Pierre Vadeboncoeur says in the work mentioned yesterday, the choice between federalism and independence has become "our main political problem," "an important subject," "a crucial question." Similarly, this is how men like René Lévesque and Jacques Parizeau have put the question which must be resolved on April 29 before the electors. Henceforth this is how the problem will be seen by thousands of Québécois.

'It is vital therefore that next Wednesday the people of Quebec state clearly whether they are for or against retaining the federal link as it now stands. Secondly, supposing they are in favour of retaining the federal link, they must say which of the three other parties is best suited to ensure the political development of Quebec within a Canadian framework.'

Mr. Ryan himself opted for the federalist option, but felt compelled to deal at length with the Péquistes:

'The case of the Parti québécois is more involved, more intricate. In its two years of existence the PQ has accomplished a colossal task and rendered immeasurable service to democracy in Quebec.

'This party has channelled countless sources of energy which would otherwise have been drawn into disgust, indifference, complete abstainment, or anarchy into democratic involvement. The party has acted as a voice for thousands of citizens drawn not solely from the ranks of those who favour self-determination, but also from the even larger band of those who feel the need for fundamental political renewal. In the democratic nature of its internal structure and the large public meetings which have marked the regular conventions, the party has demonstrated its belief in free discussion, democratic guidelines, and hard work. Its leader is an exceptional person who, because of his courage, his experience on the public scene, and his energy, is the strongest leader around. In the space of a few months he has succeeded in giving respect and credibility to an option which

| JEAN-JACQUES BERTRAND | ROBERT BOURASSA |
| UNION NATIONALE | LIBERAL |

Constitution and independence

The National Union is pledged to bring about a new Canadian constitution which would respect the fundamental rights of Quebec as the national home of French-speaking Canadians. The revision is stalled because of the rigid, intolerant and arrogant attitude of the Federal government. If after four years, negotiations are not underway, or progressing to Quebec's satisfaction, a referendum on whether Quebec should stay in Confederation will be held.

The Liberal Party wants to accelerate the negotiations to change the constitution in order to get a more precise, more efficient sharing of powers between the two levels of government to prevent duplication.

Unemployment

Create upwards of 50,000 new jobs annually during the next four years and make a complete inventory of the manpower situation. Review the needs for labor of the various sectors of the economy. More than half of the current unemployment of 9.2 per cent is attributable to the federal government's anti-inflation measures.

The first priority of my government will be the untangling of our financial mess to re-allocate money, if necessary, to job-creating investments, capital expenditures (roads, Government construction, S.G.F. investment). Our unemployment rate is at an unprecedented height. It must be curbed at all costs.

Economic development

The creation of an industrial development company to promote and attract industry to Quebec, and to oversee the merger of key industries where needed. Creation of an export information board to promote Quebec exports, and greater incentive to Quebec industries.

Economic development is as much a priority in Quebec as the creation of 100,000 new jobs. Without it, we cannot achieve our goals of solving unemployment. Development must be rational and fast. To do this we must carefully choose the priorities of our government.

Federal-Provincial

The revision of cost-sharing programs and bringing back of all such programs to exclusive Quebec jurisidiction. The return to Quebec jurisdiction of social security programs now in federal hands. The return of the $200,000,000 collected by Ottawa in the past two years of social development tax.

The National Union has used those relations for its own electoral purposes, blaming Ottawa's riding policies towards Quebec. If Prime Minister Trudeau doesn't accept our economic federalism, he is not a true federalist and Canada's future will be in danger.

RENE LÉVESQUE
PARTI QUÉBÉCOIS

CAMILLE SAMSON
CRÉDITISTE

Constitution and independence

The Parti Québécois wants Quebec to be a sovereign state – a country that will be politically independent from Canada though linked to it economically.

Quebec would take over its full responsibility for all fields which fall within its jurisdiction under the constitution. These include all direct taxation, social welfare, human rights, education and immigration. Quebec would also have control over its own financial credit. The Ralliement does not see the need for independence, we're neither federalists nor separatists – we're Créditistes.

Unemployment

The quarrels between the Ottawa and Quebec governments aggravates unemployment. It is necessary to take the instruments of economic action into our own hands and that is the only way unemployment can be reduced in Quebec. Radical reorganization of employment officers will be undertaken.

By making money available free of interest, jobs will be created. With more wage-earners the purchase of goods will be greatly increased, this leading to stepped-up productivity, which will again cut unemployment.

Economic development

There is no question of our denying the necessity and utility of certain economic links with the rest of Canada and the United States. Quebec will continue a good neighbor policy with Canada and the u.s. The party will establish a Deparment of National Economy to regroup natural resources, lands and forests, commerce and industry, tourism, fish and game.

Same as above.

Federal-Provincial

Quebec and Canada would form two separate countries within the framework of an economic and administrative alliance on a contractual and renewable basis.

The federal system can work well, provided that Ottawa can be induced to allow the province necessary control of its credit, through the establishment of an autonomous Quebec branch of the Bank of Canada.

JEAN-JACQUES BERTRAND UNION NATIONALE	ROBERT BOURASSA LIBERAL

Education

Streamlining and modernization of actual school board structures into new and more viable units. We will make CEGEP's curriculum meet the particular manpower needs of the community the CEGEP is located in.

   Adult retraining programs will be expanded and French will be better taught in the schools by training more and better qualified French teachers. Free education at the university level will be introduced gradually.

It's in an unbelievable mess. Parents are worried, students are disoriented, teachers are not paid. Education problems today are due to lack of leadership. We have to fit our graduates into the labor market, we need better information on possible opportunities.

   A Liberal government will establish permanent re-adaption centres.

French language

We will make French the priority language in Quebec without doing away with the minority language rights in education. A linguistic research centre will be established, and the greater use of French will be promoted in industry and commerce.

French must be the working language of Quebec but we don't need to break up Canada to achieve that goal. Our approach is on the working language first, education after. If people work in French, they will send their children to the French schools.

---

not so long ago was considered unacceptable and eccentric. And finally this party offers to the people of Quebec a team of candidates which includes at least twenty men of outstanding value.

   'Despite all these points in its favour – most of which are the answer to our greatest expectations, we cannot support the Parti québécois' in this election. This is why:

   '1 The fundamental proposal put forward by the PQ, that is Quebec's political separation from the rest of Canada, is premature. From now on the problem presents serious implications; above and beyond the mathematical outcome of April 29, this will be the principal achievement of the present campaign. But the time is not ripe for resolving the problem in the radical and irrevocable manner suggested by the PQ ... When one considers the present state of the economy and of public finance in Quebec, it would be ill-advised to act so radically at this time.

   '2 The PQ's political programme contains serious gaps, as we pointed out here on April 9. The new balance of power which the party suggests between the various elements of the social body are inspired by generous considerations. However, it is more radical and

| **RENE LÉVESQUE** | **CAMILLE SAMSON** |
| PARTI QUÉBÉCOIS | CRÉDITISTE |

Education

The school system will be free up to and including university level and a system of living allowances for students to include a pre-salary plan, will also be established.

The denominational school system will be restored as the base for the future so that everyone can have the sort of education he chooses.

French language

French will become the only official language. A law will make the use of French obligatory in all business. But the PQ will respect the rights of English-speaking citizens who will receive grants from the government on a percentage basis of population.

French will be the priority language, but the acquired rights of the minorities will be respected. Parents will have the freedom of choice for the type of education they want for their children.

far-reaching than it would seem at first sight. Both in the area of foreign and internal politics, the PQ's programme seems more like an idealistic forecast for the society of tomorrow than a collection of realistic proposals for the immediate future.

'3 The team of candidates offered to the public by the PQ includes several interesting names which we would like to see in Parliament. Nevertheless this list is not as well-balanced as one might expect of a group which is asking for the power to govern. The list contains too high a proportion of overly young citizens, whose experience of life and public affairs is limited ....

'4 All in all the Parti québécois is still a very young party. Within its ranks there are men of varying, sometimes conflicting, tendencies. The personality of its leaders and of a few outstanding members has so far managed to create an impression of unity. But it would appear that this unity rests on weak foundations. One feels that the real confrontations are still to come within this party. Until such time it is impossible to know clearly which way the PQ will eventually bend.

'Only a few years will be needed for this filtration – or, if you like, symbiosis – to occur.'

Dismissing the New Democratic party (à regret) and the Ralliement créditiste, Mr. Ryan observed: 'If we were to go along with a conventional wisdom which has on occasion been overlooked at great cost to Quebec, this time we should come down on the side of the Union nationale. By so doing we would avoid having a "rouge" government in Ottawa and a "rouge" government in Quebec. The ever-present risk of alliances between the members of the same political family would be circumscribed.' But conventional wisdom had to be shelved, he concluded, because the Union nationale 'does not possess the language, the analytical or working methods which suit younger generations or the new technocratical élite who have been trained in modern governmental sciences.' Only the Liberals remained:

'The Liberal party chief, Mr Bourassa, has not offered the public the outstanding team he promised at the time of his leadership campaign. He appears before the public at the head of the party which for four years has seemed to be vacillating after the enthusiasm which it initially showed for a truer democratization. He has not answered all the questions which needed to be on certain key aspects of his programme, notably in respect of the promise of 100,000 new jobs in 1971. He has not yet given sufficient guarantee that he will be firm in possible negotiations with the central government.

'And yet, of the three leaders representing those parties which are inclined to give federalism a serious chance, he has appeared as the one most capable of taking the struggle into enemy territory, of entering into dialogue with young people, of tackling and understanding problems with the technical ability required in our time of a man of state. Furthermore he has appeared as the man who is surrounded for the time being by a team of moderate youthfulness, representing various areas of activity ...

'Constitutionally speaking the Liberal party has not given definite replies to the criticisms levelled against it during the campaign. But Mr Bourassa has shown no degree of servility in so far as Ottawa is concerned. In terms which may be too concise but which are down to earth, he has stipulated those attitudes which differentiate him quite clearly from the Trudeau team. He has not tied his hands for the future. When one remembers that – to spur him on – he will have not only the Union nationale but also the Parti québécois, the risk he might present in different circumstances is considerably lessened. Once prime minister, Mr Bourassa will be well-advised (as will the rest of Canada) to see that federalism operates in accordance with the fundamental expectations of Quebec.

Lost in the constitution woods

Montreal *Gazette*, April 24, 1970

'Of the three parties with federalist tendencies, the Liberal party also seems to be the one most capable of bringing about an economic upsurge and at the same time the rationalization of public administration of which Quebec stands so much in need. Mr Bourassa possesses an excellent understanding of the mechanics of economic activity and public administration in North America. He understands the language of figures. Without any hesitation he admits the necessity for private enterprise and at the same time is fully acquainted with the new forms that the state's intervention in the economy takes in our time. We have more confidence, for the immediate future, in his approach, than in the Union nationale's improvisations or in Messrs Parizeau's or Lévesque's overconfident equations.'

The verdict

'Today this feels like a splendid country,' shouted the *Globe and Mail* on April 30, for 'the Province of Quebec is alive and well in Canada.' More soberly the *Montreal Star* assured its up-tight English-Canadian readers that 'Quebec has granted us a second chance.' The *Gazette* saw the Liberal victory as 'a vote of confidence in Canada.' 'Quebec voters respond in a fashion reassuring to Canadians in all parts of the country,' echoed the *Winnipeg Free Press*. On the surface, at least, the electoral verdict seemed to justify such optimistic conclusions (1966 figures are bracketed):

	Seats	Percentage of total vote
Liberals	72 (50)	41.8 (47)
Parti québécois	7	23
Union nationale	17 (56)	19.6 (41)
Ralliement créditiste	12	11.1
Others	0 (2)	4.5 (12)

The federalist rejoicing was understandable, but overdone. For the Liberal sweep alone did nothing to remove the serious economic and social problems; and in it were seeds of further antagonisms and potentially dangerous political reorganization.

'In giving you their support,' wired Mr Trudeau to M. Bourassa, 'it is clear that the people of Quebec have accepted your option: the path of work, of reason, and of confidence.' It was equally clear, however, that the Liberal share of the popular vote declined sharply, despite the obvious increase in the turnout of English-speaking or non-French Quebeckers. Far clearer was that a troubled and discontented electorate had gone to the polls on April 29. Never strong in the cities, the Union nationale was virtually wiped out by the urban voters. Rural malaise found its outlet in a massive swing to the Ralliement créditiste, which won nine seats from the Union nationale and three from the Liberals. Moreover, in fourteen additional UN seats the Créditistes, often running second to the victorious Liberals, gave Bourassa the seat by attracting thousands of UN supporters.

For several years before the 1970 election students of Quebec separatism had pointed out that a significant fraction – sometimes estimated at 50 per cent – of nationalists espousing the separatist cause simply felt that M. Lévesque was a better leader than his opponents or that the Parti québécois had a domestic programme better suited to the needs of Quebec society. Pre-election polls revealed much the same thing. Undoubtedly that programme was designed to appeal to the urban voter, and whether it was nationalism or radicalism that was so appealing, the Parti québécois made a remarkable showing in urban Quebec. In Montreal's depressed east end it swept five seats from the Union nationale and one from the Liberals. Elsewhere in the city it ran second to the Liberals in every riding, including the Anglophone areas. Excluding the four overwhelmingly English constituencies, the Liberals secured only 373,757 votes to 249,251 for the Parti québécois. To the north and south of Montreal, it often ran a strong second, and lost Fabre by only ninety-one votes. In more than twenty-five constituencies outside Montreal the Parti québécois polled more than one-fifth of the vote, showing signs of real strength in Quebec City, the depressed lower south shore, and the north – where it won Saguenay from the Liberals and ran second in Lac St-Jean and Jonquière. Only in the highly overrepresented rural counties southeast of Montreal and in the areas bordering Ontario did it show little strength.

Federalists and English Canadians observed that seven out of ten voters had rejected the separatist solution. Including the Union nationale as resolutely federalist (despite its ambiguous position on the constitutional future) the conclusion was as accurate as election generalizations can be. Separatist analysts were not content with such gross statistics, however. Even on election night it was clear that English-speaking Quebec had voted solidly Liberal. The charges that M. Bourassa owed his majority to English-speaking Quebec – and that M. Lévesque had been defeated by the Anglophones in Laurier – were repeated in the days that passed, and were finally argued with statistical documentation in Bernard Smith's *Le Coup d'Etat du Avril 29* (which appeared in the autumn).

Breaking the City of Montreal and a number of other constituencies down by percentage of French Canadians and non-French Canadians, and also breaking the constituencies down into areas ranging from 80 to 90 per cent to 0 to 10 per cent non-French Canadian, Mr Smith easily demonstrated that English Canadians had voted Liberal and that the gap between the Liberals and the Parti québécois often varied with the percentage of non-French Canadians in the constituency. Only in nine of the thirty-eight seats in Montreal and its environs, Smith's figures argued, did the Liberals secure a higher percentage of the French-Canadian vote that the Péquistes. (One was Mercier, where Bourassa secured an estimated three hundred more French-Canadian votes than his opponent Pierre Bourgault, but emerged with a comfortable margin of more than three thousand thanks to a solid English vote.) Taking the province as a whole Smith concluded that French-speaking Quebec had given 32.6 per cent of its support to the Liberals, 28.7 to the PQ, 24.2 to the UN, and 14.5 per cent to others. The decision in twenty ridings, he declared, was determined by the non-French-Canadian vote. The conclusion was clear: without those twenty seats the Liberals in the National Assembly would have been in a minority, as they were in the popular vote.

Never before in modern Quebec's history had the line between many French Canadians and the non-French Canadians been so firmly and clearly drawn, unless it was the provincial election of 1939. The conflicts over separatism, and perhaps equally over language and educational policy, had born fruit. The issue was personalized and the results more bitter on election night when it was clear that the Italian-Canadian voters of Laurier had deserted Lévesque and refused to give their support to an Italian UN candidate to vote solidly Liberal, and that in Ahuntsic non-French Canadians had narrowly defeated Jacques Parizeau. Commenting on the Brinks affair and the joyful reactions in Montreal's English dailies, M. Parizeau warned that 'these people are just waving a red flag in front of a fuming bull ... they are really asking for trouble.' Not only were the internal tensions made more acute, but the election results led many to question the democratic or representative system. As Parizeau exclaimed: 'God help us ... You see it is not my defeat nor that of René Lévesque that is important ... It's the defeat of our arguments in favour of the parliamentary system.'

While some ultra-nationalists were prepared to spend four years strengthening the PQ base and preparing for the predictable takeover in the next election, others were not. René Lévesque himself cautioned moderation and claimed an immense victory on election night, but by August his tone was different in an interview with the Canadian Press (*Ottawa Citizen*, August 22):

'Q: How do you interpret the election results? Some saw massive approval for federalism in the election.

'A: First a fact that is terribly flagrant. It's that 95 per cent of the Anglophone bloc – I studied enough polls, including Laurier – voted Liberal ... Even little old ladies on stretchers were hauled out in the end-of-régime panic, as if it were the end of the Roman Empire. They got them out and they manipulated them to the hilt ...

'There's another striking thing about the election. It's that the defeated candidates we are most sorry about, men like Parizeau and Morin ... were often defeated only by the vote of the Anglophone ghetto. They had bigger French majorities ... than those who were elected. In other words they got a bigger percentage of the French vote than those who won. That's the disturbing second fact considered from the point of view of the possibilities of the democratic process.

'Is Montreal going to be annexed sufficiently year after year to make it impossible for the majority group in Quebec to win an increasing number of ridings at Montreal? This is the danger of assimilation, which is increasing. The electoral map will figure in this. We'll see what kind of work will be done in reforming the map. But you know things could get pretty damned serious if the will, becoming clearer and clearer of an ethnic majority, is blocked by an ethnic minority within Quebec.

'I don't have to draw pictures for you. It can become very grave ... In other countries this kind of thing provokes explosions.

'Q: Has your attitude towards Quebec's English-speaking minority changed since the election?

'A: I want to be very clear about this ... I know very well that your interview will be reproduced honestly. That happens once every six months in a sort of sea of propaganda organized by your English mass media. That doesn't change things very much. It's the typical good old Anglo-Saxon method; "Let's give him a day in court."

'I'm not talking about you. I'm talking about those who manipulate your information and your propaganda in the English media. I was brought up half in English and half in French and have lived in English as much as I have lived in French. Yet I have never experienced such disgust ... as the disgust I experienced because of the way information was manipulated in the Anglo-Saxon Establishment at Montreal with its propaganda media, its disrespect for a population which is treated like "natives."

'Q: Can the independence of Quebec really be achieved democratically? Considering the makeup of the population and the electoral map, it seems that the answer is no.

'A: It's possible eventually that the answer will be no. It's possible only we can't accept it ... I think that the last democratic chance will be in the next election ... And if there is the same manipulation of elections – and I'm talking more about manipulation of the minds than of the electoral system – it's obvious that the conscious minority ... is going to have the almost irresistible temptation to blow up the institutions. But I honestly believe there is still a chance.'

Lévesque and the October crisis

Seven weeks later the FLQ found the temptation to blow up institutions irresistible. As the crisis wore on and the army approached Montreal, Lévesque drafted a document urging the governments to negotiate the freedom of Cross and Laporte for the release of the so-called political prisoners – that is, terrorists who were in jail for criminal acts. Fifteen men accepted his invitation to attend a meeting at the Holiday Inn on October 14 where they approved the statement which, when revised by Lévesque and Claude Ryan, ran as follows:

'The Cross-Laporte affair is primarily a Quebec drama. One of the two hostages is a citizen of Quebec, the other a diplomat whose functions made him a temporary citizen with the same rights to respect for his life and to his dignity as a man as us all.

'On the other hand, the people of the FLQ are a marginal section of the same Quebec. But they still form part of our reality, because extremism is a part of the social structure, even if it indicates a serious condition and can put the social structure in mortal peril.

'The destiny of two human lives, the reputation and collective honour of our society, the obvious danger of a political and social degradation that this society is presently facing, all this makes it clear to us that the responsibility for finding a solution and applying it quite rightly lies primarily with Quebec.

'We feel that certain attitudes outside Quebec, the last and most unbelievable of which was that of Premier Robarts of Ontario, plus the rigid – almost military – atmosphere we see in Ottawa, run the risk of reducing Quebec and its government to tragic ineffectualness. Super-human effort [is needed] to agree to bargain and compromise. In this respect, we believe that Quebec and its government really hold the re-sponsibility and the moral mandate, and are the real custodians of the facts and the climate of opinion which allow them to make knowledge-able decisions.

'Especially as, particularly in certain non-Quebec quarters, we fear the terrible temptation of the worst type of politics, in other words the idea that Quebec in chaos and disorder would at last be easy to con-trol by any available means.

'This is why, forgetting the difference of opinion we have on a num-ber of subjects, solely conscious for the moment of being Québécois and therefore totally involved, we wish to give our complete support to the intention announced Sunday evening by the Bourassa govern-ment, which means basically our strongest support for negotiating an exchange of the two hostages for the political prisoners. This must be accomplished despite and against all obstruction from outside Que-bec, which necessarily implies the positive co-operation of the federal government.

'And we urgently invite all the citizens who share our point of view to make it known publicly as quickly as possible.

'The signatories of the statement are: René Lévesque, president of the Parti québécois; Alfred Rouleau, president of l'Assurance-vie-Desjardins; Marcel Pépin, president of CSN; Louis Laberge, president of the FTQ [Fédération des travailleurs du Québec]; Jean-Marc Kiro-uac, president of the UCC [Union catholique des cultivateurs]; Claude Ryan, director of Le Devoir; Jacques Parizeau, president of the exec-utive council of the Parti québécois; Fernand Daoust, secretary gen-eral of the FTQ; Yvan Charbonneau, president of the CEQ [Corporation des enseignants du Québec]; Mathias Rioux, president of l'Alliance des professeurs of Montreal; Camille Laurin, parliamentary leader of the Parti québécois; Guy Rocher, sociology professor at l'Université de Montréal; Fernand Dumont, director of l'Institut supérieur des sci-ences humaines at l'Université Laval; Paul Bélanger, political science professor at l'Université Laval; Raymond Laliberté, ex-president of CEQ; Marcel Rioux, anthropology professor at l'Université de Montréal.'

But the governments preferred to use the army and the War Measures

Act rather than capitulate to the FLQ, and Lévesque at once issued a
lengthy statement.

. 'Quebec no longer has a government.'
The bit of country over which we had any control has been swept
away by the first hard blow. The Bourassa cabinet has stepped down
and is no more than a puppet in the hands of the federal leaders.
'It is now quite obvious that – right from the beginning of this tragic
period which began with Mr Cross' kidnapping – the only part played
by the government has been as walk-on. We are unfortunately forced
to believe that even while the pseudo-negotiations opened last Sunday by Mr Bourassa were going on he was, according to an agreement, merely acting as the tool of a policy which had been formulated
without referring to him, and that he adopted a compromising attitude
while knowing all the time about the rigid line which Ottawa had chosen; that in fact he had been preparing the necessary climate, meanwhile letting the situation continue and deteriorate while pretending to
hesitate, and that, finally, last night, it was he who sanctioned the extreme steps taken by the Trudeau régime, whereby all of Quebec is
put under military occupation until next spring.

'... Nor can we help thinking and saying that this degradation of
Quebec was intended – quite consciously by some and instinctively
by others.

'The guiding factors have taken two extreme forms.

'Firstly there is the thoroughly official, legally recognized federal establishment, backed by economic and other forces. It was from here
that the first murmur was heard of the likelihood of resorting to all
means including military force for the purpose of keeping Quebec,
and, if need be, putting it in its place.

'For years it has been in this area that attempts have been made to
stifle the hopes of the Québécois, howsoever moderately ambitious
they might have been, swamping them in the undergrowth of committees, meetings, and eternal new beginnings. We are obliged to say
that from the highest levels of this establishment orders were given for
that non-stop flow of propaganda the aim of which was to disfigure
and ridicule every aspect of democratic nationalism in Quebec at all
costs, and which knew no bounds, resorting to the worst type of slan-
der in order to prove subversion and terrorism.

'At the other extreme let us hope that those very people who threw
themselves body and soul into a career of subversion and terrorism –

both of which are so tragically contrary to the best interests of our people – may at least realize now that they have in fact been the fore-runners of the military régime thereby endangering the basic rights of all Québécois.

'Finally, we do not know how large the revolutionary army is or was, nor the extent of their power to create disorder and anarchy. Until we receive proof to the contrary – and every responsible citizen should demand this proof and be given it as soon as possible if it exists or else drop out from a self-respecting society – until we receive proof to the contrary we will believe that such a minute, numerically unimpor-tant fraction is involved, that rushing into the enforcement of the War Measures Act was a panicky and altogether excessive reaction, espe-cially when you think of the inordinate length of time they want to maintain this régime.

'The most worrying thing – and this might also reveal quite specific and even more inadmissible intentions, is that the arrests, the deten-tions (whether preventive or otherwise) and the searches, have taken on the proportions of a full police operation right across Quebec.

'We believe that in this respect at least (which is the most urgent) we can call on all Québécois, especially those who are highly placed, fully confident that at this time of such unprecedented gravity we will find enough solidarity and calm democratic strength to prevent this dangerous climate from degenerating into blind repression ...

'In view of the extremes which have for all practical purposes caused the destruction of our government, Quebec's democrats must overcome their differences of opinion immediately and find the means or the organizations for building the moral power necessary to defend our basic liberties and, at the same time, all our hopes for the future.'

Addressing a regional Parti québécois conference on November 8 Lévesque charged the federal government with fascist manipulation of Quebec.

'For them the kidnappings have served merely as a pretext, nothing more than to stifle the people by manipulation. Hitler didn't come to power by using force ...

'However, men like Marchand, Trudeau, and Drapeau and the peo-ple around them have taken advantage of the October events to seize Quebec and turn the Quebec government into a puppet.

'This was a manipulation of the people of Quebec and Trudeau behaved like a fascist manipulator. Fascism means a taste for absolute power which suffers no answers, the coercion of outsiders into the ranks. Trudeau justified his War Measures by saying: tomorrow it could be a farmer, a child (he mentioned children twice), the manager of a savings bank. All that to manipulate the people. The more nervous he is, the more broadcasts Trudeau makes. There were calculated errors, when he mentioned people who don't agree (like me and Ryan, who were both for negotiation) and wondering whether we weren't in sympathy with the FLQ. That's all the same type of dirty fascist manipulation as Caouette uses. Both of them can be ranked together as fascist manipulators ...

'We don't have to make any excuses for what has happened. We tore our hearts out trying to uproot the FLQ and redirect it. But who poisoned democracy? Trudeau, the federal "gang" and federal finance which manipulated the April elections, which tried to crush the PQ even though we wanted to avoid any violence. These professional hypocrites tried to make out FLQ and PQ were one then. Today some of the political slobs are holding a hand out to the PQ when five months ago they did everything to destroy a decision which made good collective sense.

'Now they are reaping what they sowed. The PQ doesn't have to make any excuses. It just has to make itself legally accepted as a legitimate party while waiting for an end to be made to a system which encourages unhealthy FLQ extremism on the one hand and displaced persons like Trudeau on the other.'

As the year ended, observers speculated on the effects of the October crisis on the future of the Parti québécois.

The *Winnipeg Free Press* (October 19) had no doubts: 'The murder of Mr. Laporte should, if there is any justice, sound the death knell of the separatist movement in Quebec. If it does, his death, tragic as it has been, will not have been in vain.' Quite clearly the *Free Press* was incapable of distinguishing between the Péquistes and Félquistes, or of accepting any middle ground between hawks and doves. Nevertheless, the Parti québécois may have suffered because of the crisis.

Gilles Lalande, a Montreal political scientist, declared that 'the separatist wave has just died,' because FLQ, FRAP, and others had so clearly linked ultra-radicalism with ultra-nationalism. In his interview with Louis Martin on 'Format 60,' Prime Minister Trudeau observed that 'some separatist leaders and many others have supported, you might say, the objectives of the FLQ' and 'at least one FLQ aim: a government agreement to free prisoners.' In reply to Martin's question 'That makes them accomplices, does it not?' the Prime Minister said: 'Not at all ... I find ... and I am answering your question ... perhaps they identified themselves in the public mind not with the use of violence but with the demands of those who were using it.' Mr Trudeau's discretion was not shared by M. Choquette during the November 13 debate in the Assembly. Vigorously attacking the Parti québécois, he asked: 'But in fact might these preachers of non-violence be hawks disguised under the convenient feathers of doves? Behind these all too easy escapist solutions of the Parti québécois and its leader in particular, might there not exist a calculated political move aimed at undermining present democratic institutions? This seems quite obvious to me.'

Yet if some were driven from separatism by the ambiguity of its leaders or the rhetoric of Choquette, others may have been driven closer by the seeming futility of the decade-old struggle to improve conditions in the province. On several occasions Claude Ryan said that the crisis forced a basic re-examination of Quebec society and its relations with Ottawa. In a November 9 editorial he denied that he had moved over to René Lévesque, but wrote that two basic questions had to be answered:

'1. Might not the types of political and social structures under which we live be responsible, to any extent yet to be determined, for the continual crises which we have witnessed?

'2. Will these same structures be capable, in the case of fresh crises threatening on the horizon, of bringing about peace, liberty, and prosperity – without which political life is hardly worth living – for our society?'

Although Mr Ryan promised to keep his readers informed as he moved along the road, it appeared to many that he had already reached his destination. It may be that many others, hoping above all to find peace in a troubled Quebec, had also. And in English Canada there were some nationalists of the left, like Abraham Rotstein, who seemed to see the October crisis as the prelude to an armed confrontation if Quebec reached separatism by democratic means. 'We must now travel in tandem,' he wrote in the *Canadian Forum* (January 1971) 'to create in English Canada active legal, political and institutional channels that support and foster Quebec's legitimate aspirations. It is our only hope of mitigating the impact of the collision which looms ahead.'

1971

Union support

For a few days in 1971 it appeared that the long road towards constitutional reform was nearing its end. The work of the constitutional
conference and the expenditure of millions of dollars in man-hours
came to fruition in the celebrated Victoria Charter. The charter was so
typically Canadian – free of rhetoric or even of inspired prose. Basically it left the old machine of the federal state much as it was, removing a few redundant parts and adding a few new bearings to entrench
language rights and giving Quebec and Ontario a veto over constitutional amendments. Yet within a week the charter was dead as Premier Bourassa faced a hastily organized common front of nationalists
in Quebec who believed the charter did not go nearly far enough in
the direction of decentralization and/or special status for Quebec.
When he did as he was bid and 'dit non,' the country moved back to
ad hoc federalism, almost with a sign of relief, a federalism that increasingly obstructed concerted attacks on national and regional
problems and slowly, but seemingly surely, drove many French-Canadian intellectuals with their distaste for anglophone pragmatism towards the philosophic purity of a separate state. The Bloc québécois
surfaced briefly in the summer with the declared intention of running
separatist candidates in the next federal election, an objective supported by 53 per cent of Montreal francophones according to one survey. The FLQ continued its fitful terrorism, despite a massive crack-
down in October, but Pierre Vallières, one of the philosophers of the
revolution, renounced violence and declared his support for the Parti
québécois.

At a July 27 press conference Prime Minister Trudeau said that he felt
that 'separatism is not stronger than it was three or four years ago.
There may be an increased polarization. In other words, those who
were separatists three or four years ago may feel even more strongly
for separatism now, but I don't think their number has substantially
increased.' Such an optimistic conclusion was certainly borne out by
the apparent fall-off in card-carrying members of the Parti québécois,
but there were too many signs of what was at least a movement towards separatism, arising from strains in the social and political status
quo, to warrant too optimistic a conclusion.

Léon Dion, Laval's distinguished political scientist and the co-di-
rector of research for the B and B Commission, had been less optimistic when he appeared before the Senate House Committee on the
Constitution on March 30. Still committed to a federal solution to the
Canadian problem, Professor Dion warned that without measures far
more radical and imaginative than those so far undertaken, and without a willingness on the part of Anglophone Canada to pay a heavy
price, the country would have to accept 'as inevitable' the separatism
of Quebec. His proposed measures included the clear right of self-determination to the point of independence for Quebec and any other
province, a large percentage of unilingual Quebeckers to preserve an
endangered language and culture, massive institutional (rather than
personal) bilingualism in the federal civil service, and major jurisdic-
tional and administrative decentralization by the federal government.
Canadians must end the sterile discussion of 'abstract concepts' such
as two nations or special status, Mr. Dion insisted.

'No power in the world can stop the French-speaking Québécois
from seeing themselves as a unique society and nation, separate from
the over-all reality of Canada. On the other hand, despite all their
good will, few English-speaking Canadians manage to see themselves
as a special nation within the Canadian reality. Furthermore, the
Québécois understand this perfectly well; the best-informed have already consigned the idea of the "two nations" to oblivion, or soon
will. The same goes for the notions of "special status for Quebec"
and of "associated states." Let there be agreement on the basic elements first and we will come up with a name for them later on.'

'Concluding his brief Professor Dion warned English Canada and
the federal government to think seriously before rejecting radical and
costly solutions. But he could make no promises for Quebec:

'As for the French-speaking Québécois, even in the best of all possible contexts it is impossible to predict what their eventual choice will be. Some have committed themselves firmly to separation. Others are undecided. Still others are panic-stricken. An economic upswing, increased participation in the country's political life, or a radical change in their situation in Confederation, would be liable to change their attitude.

'No one knows whether, tomorrow, the remaining will to co-exist will be victorious over the will to separate.'

'When even the most pious lose their faith, the high priests of Ottawa should be giving their dogmas another look' wrote an approving Claude Lemelin of *Le Devoir* (April 2).

'Prime Minister Trudeau observed at a December 22 press conference that 'there are certainly people in the province of Quebec who are trying to polarize opinion and lead us into class warfare.' Léon Dion pointed to the congruence of the radical and nationalistic forces in Quebec before the Senate House Committee. Certainly the increasing radicalization of the trade unions, the adoption of starkly socialistic manifestos based on a marxist analysis of the roots of Quebec's ills by the union leadership (although the views of the membership were never made clear), the overt support by the leadership of all nationalistic causes – whether the Victoria Charter or English-language education – and the frequent association of the central unions and the Parti québécois suggested a polarization of opinion that could strengthen the nationalist-separatist cause.

During the summer the Corporation des enseignants de Québec adopted a study document calling for the overthrow of the capitalist system and the creation of a socialist Quebec. The principal author of the document was Robert Delorme, who before joining the staff of CEQ was a philosophy teacher influenced by Herbert Marcuse. Mr. Delorme and other left-wing members of the executive, who called themselves 'les camarades,' argued that teachers should be paid from corporation taxes because they were hired to teach the ideology of the capitalist system: 'The negotiations could bring up the whole question of the capitalist system and unmask it,' Delorme told William Johnson of the *Globe and Mail* (December 25). 'It would be the tip of the lance, the first blow struck against the system.' The CEQ undertook a major study and political education programme among its members and set up a network of politically active committees.

On September 8 the central council of the CNTU adopted a document entitled 'Quebec has no future in the present economic system.'

While the study document was silent on the question of separatism, the only conclusion that could be reached from it and a second one in October, 'Let us rely on our own resources,' was that Quebec had to be an independent socialist state. In a long and rambling speech at the Quebec Federation of Labour [FTQ] convention on November 30 Louis Laberge called for a socialist Quebec and a united front to oppose the capitalist system. M. Laberge spoke warmly of René Lévesque, despite his refusal to join the La Presse demonstration a few weeks before, and argued that despite its too liberal ideology the PQ was the best for the workers. The workshops saw near unanimity on a socialist manifesto and for a common front of all labour organizations to achieve political and social ends. The convention overruled a workshop decision to oppose either massive participation in a political party or the formation of a new one, and gave the governing council what Laberge called the flexibility and manoeuvrability to consider either of the alternatives. On the last day the convention voted approval of Quebec's right of self-determination including independence if it was achieved 'in accordance with the needs and aspirations of the workers,' and while rejecting an endorsement of separatism refused to reiterate the FTQ's previous opposition to it. The convention also declared that French should be the only official working language in the province. Finally, it approved a common front of the three major unions and gave the executive a mandate to call a general strike. On December 14 the FTQ leaders met with members of the CNTU and CEQ to work out the details of a common front.

The sudden radicalization of the hitherto moderate Laberge was partly attributed to the October 29 riot at La Presse when between eight and twelve thousand demonstrators clashed with police. Police had barricaded the area around La Presse, but despite Laberge's pacific efforts demonstrators attempted to mount the barricades and one attempted to ram it with a truck. Police swept out from behind the buildings to disperse the rioters, and before the evening was over several buses had been burned, many cars damaged, eight policemen were injured, seventy demonstrators were taken to hospital, and thirty were arrested. During the riot Michèle Gauthier, a frequent participant in such demonstrations, died of an asthma attack. Her husband, a Radio-Canada news editor, called it 'assassination, pure and simple,' while Laberge termed it 'murder, a real murder.' At a mass meeting at the Forum of twelve thousand on November 2 Laberge warned: 'But the next time not all the victims will be on our side.'

Toronto Star, November 30, 1971

The radicalization of the trade union leadership and their movement towards political action provided René Lévesque and the PQ with both an opportunity and a danger. The opportunity was the prospect of the machinery and means for elections, as well as members, but the danger was that the polarization of opinion and the open advocacy of class warfare could drive away the middle class péquistes and many moderate trade unionists. Lévesque's refusal to move radically to the left had been a continual source of trouble for him in the past, and became even more so in 1971 as he faced pressure both from inside and outside the party. M. Lévesque had contemplated resigning, but on January 9 he announced that he would remain and contest the leadership, believing not only that he had a useful role to play but that his departure 'could have consequences that might "dirty" the political atmosphere "even further" and stir up new waves of violence.'

At the February 26-29 convention Lévesque easily defeated the symbolic opposition of André Larocque, but only with difficulty could he restrain the twelve hundred delegates from abolishing minority schools in an independent Quebec. The party executive was also able to keep the left wing in line, and the resolutions reflected the moderate position on economic and social issues that it had held since the beginning. Nevertheless, there were voices urging a radicalization of the party, and Pierre Bourgault, who had been held at arm's length by the party leaders since the merger with the defunct RIN, was elected to the party executive.

But the socio-economic orientation of the party continued to pose internal problems as some of the left wing wanted it to move towards the radical positions being adopted by the major trade unions and some citizens' committees. The issue finally broke over the October 29 *La Presse* demonstration. Only by a vote of 6 to 5 was Lévesque able to persuade the party executive not to participate in a demonstration which predictably would lead to violence. Supporting Lévesque were Jacques Parizeau, Charles Tremblay, MNA, and three party members. Opposed were four members of the Assembly and Pierre Bourgault. Robert Burns and Lucien Lessard, both members of the Assembly, indicated they sided with the minority.

Rumours of discontent broke open in *Québec Presse* (November 7) when Louis Fournier quoted Robert Burns as stating that 'we haven't heard the last of that.' The party, he declared, 'still has much to do to get close to the working people and their genuine concerns. As far as I am concerned, the PQ should be clearly on the side of the exploited, and not attempt to gain power under false pretences.' Burns admitted he was disgusted by the 6 to 5 decision, on which he did not vote since he had indicated that he intended to march and would not consider himself bound by the decision, and added: 'We must ask ourselves whether the Parti québécois is not simply a slightly more advanced wing of the Liberal Party or other comparable old parties. In any case the grass-roots reaction, especially in the Montreal ridings where we have been returned, is a clear indication that the party was mistaken. There is no reason for us to be surprised at seeing several ridings in rebellion against the leadership and hearing talk of dissension.' And on November 9 André Larocque's *Défis au parti québécois*, a critique of Lévesque's leadership and the party structure, was scheduled to appear.

René Lévesque took the initiative and called a November 8 press conference where, according to Michel Roy (*Le Devoir,* November 9), he 'denied the reports published on Sunday in *Québec Presse* ...; [he] stated that Robert Burns, PQ member for Maisonneuve who has just compared his party to "a slightly more advanced wing of the Liberal Party," can "go if he wants to"; issued the same invitation to the "elements who supported the FLQ last year" and that are attempting to "infiltrate" the PQ; strongly deplored the actions of the union chiefs who "are in the process of alienating the workers from any true political awareness"; recalled to their responsibilities those who, "by beatification of the terrorists," are pushing young people to commit senseless acts and "waste their education"; emphasized, finally, that the Parti québécois has committed itself to the achievement of independence, "which is only a means," in order to bring about reforms "by democratic ways": and that this "bet will be honoured" in spite of those who don't believe in it.'

But a press conference was inadequate, and on November 14 the executive called a meeting of the 150-man national council for November 28. The meetings were closed to the press, but clearly René Lévesque received overwhelming support. The council adopted a resolution imposing discipline on local groups, but not prohibiting individual dissidence of opinion. It also approved a lengthy statement, written by Lévesque, which while outlining its position and orientation provided an excellent commentary on the turbulence in Quebec:

'We believe the moment of truth is coming and that this moment will truly be, if only enough of us want it and prepare for it as we must, the dawn of an age of national freedom combined with productive social and economic change.

'We also observe, however, as is quite natural at the close of any regime, problems growing steadily worse, an economic situation more
disastrous now than ever, and the corruption of moribund institutions
and the classes that profit from them adding to conflict and injustice.
We feel all this and suffer from it as much as anyone else. With all our
strength, and from every platform we can use, we must keep on denouncing this state of affairs, and, even more importantly, explain it so
that its causes as well as its cures can be understood. We must try to
influence the policies of the day for the better, since the smallest mor-
sel of reform will always be prized by those who need it; and at the
same time, we must as always apply ourselves to developing and promoting a programme for change, the only limits of which are those imposed on us by the aspirations and the reality of Quebec. This is the
moment of all moments, while confusion spreads in so many minds,
that political action must try to pierce the darkness like a beacon,
watching over the stability and solidity of that rock on which Quebec
will soon be able to find a solid and democratic base for its move into
the future.

'Less than ever before, then, even if temptation is strong, is this the
time to give in to the bad counsels of fear, impatience, impulsiveness.
Nothing could be more futile than to rush headlong into rash ventures
and agitation which can have no result but the hardening of the regime and its continuance under pressure to await eruptions of the
most devastating kind. All the more so as, since October, even since
April, 1970, openly or surreptitiously, by commission as by omission,
the political leaders and their manipulators are clearly seen to want no
more than to poison the atmosphere while they wait for the first auspi-
cious moment to clamp the lid back on the pot ...

'Nothing could better suit our evangelists of the *tabula rasa* who do
their croaking in the side-chapels of the wishful-revolution, or again,
that doctrinaire platoon of the far left that never marches but to the
fascism of that extreme. In their wake are seen bobbing the clique of
patriot-anarchists and plain troublemakers who surface only when
there is the prospect of a long bout of the politics of the worst. Among
us, as among most modern peoples, they are the rear-guard of a su-
perseded nihilism, having no objective but the most unattainable uto-
pia (since anything that can be attained is a deadly bore), no method
but endless infiltration and agitation, no plan but to blow up the works
and, "after that we'll see." Their consciences are impregnable, im-
mune, for instance, to any sense of responsibility for the many adoles-

cents who, drained by sterile revolutionary careerism, may waste their years of training in blind confrontation or even, as is seen more and more often, disappear into childish "cells" where they can lose their futures and their very lives.

'These people would barely weigh in the balance, were it not for the fact that their extremism occasionally threatens infection to the mass of generous souls left open, by fleeting but exciting moments or by happenings more dramatic or exemplary than the average, to the delusion of the short-cut, and in particular that delusion featuring a miraculous metamorphosis of the collectivity that is supposed to bloom here suddenly as it has never done anywhere else in the world. They forget the lack of real political awareness among a host of their fellow-citizens, shut their eyes to the ever-present danger of reaction and backsliding that haunts all societies in transition, and make their provisional leap to glory like so many missiles, without checking to see that there will be a place to land when they return ... So it is that they can fling themselves wholesale into a problematic of the year 2000, passing in anticipation right over the time that should still be spent understanding and educating the society of today and aiding it in its painful progress.

'Such persons are to be found in all movements or organizations that have any contact with situations left to rot and with people damaged by them. We have our full share, often among our most devoted supporters. It would be a pity for our political choice and for the necessary changes to which this choice alone can open a workable path, if these passing phases deprived us of their support.

'However, it is terribly wearing, and distressing to see so much time and energy lost to the lure of *ad hoc* confrontations which call forth what must be described as minimum effort.

'This is inevitable, no doubt. Group freedom and responsibility, never before experienced, are dizzying when in sight and almost within reach; and it is easy to fantasize that they can be enjoyed in advance, that a society not yet its own can be redefined on the quiet. This is the case especially in Quebec, where the national struggle for emancipation must be waged amid the usual chaos of a social revolution. We must expect people to move more or less consciously from one to the other, sometimes as if the two were mutually exclusive. But we have to find the means of carrying them on together, remembering that without national freedom we will have neither the maturity nor the necessary equipment to complete any process of social, economic or cultural renewal that is not to be deceptive or stunted.

'In these circumstances, the historic challenge that awaits us will require constant attention to balance and clarity. The point is to make as
few false steps as possible as we advance along a road that is mined
by the two extremisms, that of the regime, and that, equally aggres-
sive, of the adventurers.

'In a society that is a great collective consumer of "images," we
have done our best since the beginning to maintain an image that is
as much decency and perseverance as it is daring and renewal.

'We make no claim to success, as the appeasement of these elements would require: far from it. Worsening problems, trumped-up
crises, and the increasing growth of awareness force us to check our
approach constantly so as to bring it as much as possible into line
with changing realities and changing thinking. It is still vital, however,
to do so thoughtfully, not letting ourselves be rushed and not trying to
rush others.

'We agree that the pace must be quickened, for Quebec not only
needs but in fact now seems able to work out an original plan for its
own development – on condition, nonetheless, that the plan takes
note of certain facts that will always be 'stubborn,' having to do with
values and priorities in the choice of objectives, and of the unflagging
preparation required to make these objectives clear and acceptable.

'We have a year before us until our next convention, which has a
good chance of being a pre-election one. This is a year during which
we have rightly decided that one of our top priorities should be re-ex-
amined and that we must develop and deepen our platform, which has
not been reviewed seriously since 1969. The Executive Council hopes
to be able to submit soon, for party consideration, a group of proposals that would allow us to make another forward step, especially in the
social and economic areas. Everyone should become involved, helping to define and particularly to give as much concreteness and ra-
tionality as possible to a collective plan which we may have to put into
action before very long. One thing is sure: this plan must be brought
fairly closely into line with the Québécois' actual needs and general
aspirations, so that it can be carried forward with the same enthusiasm and effectiveness that helped the party implant the choice for independence.

'We will only reach our goal, however, if every time it seems possible that we might be forgetting it, we go back to our commitment to
develop and lead to victory a popular party, whose door must remain
wide open, but which as a result, more than any other party, should

constantly be shoring up the accepted discipline and loyalty of its supporters and especially its elected leadership. Only in this way will we be able, in full command of the facts and in constant communication, to gear the style and rhythm of our activities to the pace of events.

'Let us have a commitment also to exclude ruthlessly all forms of violence and even vague flirtations with violence, not only because they are in fundamental opposition to our way of doing things, but also because they are both immoral in human terms and futureless politically. For heaven's sake let us at the same time be ware of the slippery slope represented by a certain type of radical demogoguery, all slick with clichés and slogans as inflammatory as they are simplistic, in which everything is totally white or black, and liable to draw a good many minds into the mesh that takes them unawares to violence.

'And a commitment to rally as soon as possible, by persuasion and the strength of a conviction that is as informed, infectious and fraternal as possible, a majority of Québécois to the changes we propose. The first and most consequential of these changes – the point of departure for all the others – being national independence, we must try to reach all our people in all classes and regions, avoiding doctrinaire and artificial factionalism that will only weaken us, excluding from our efforts only those clearly allied with the groups and interests that wrongly exploit us.

'Of course, there are groups in the population who should stand as our interlocutors and be a sort of privileged clientele. First of those are the least equipped – those lacking a voice or having too little to make themselves heard, and lacking too the means to protect themselves. As one day the government we want to be, so now the party we are, we should make it a point of honour to serve first the forgotten. Next are the workers of Quebec, a great number of them in unions, but a greater number unorganized. To them we owe our support if we are to deserve theirs in return.

'With the unionized workers and their organizations we share a basic objective, that of changing and humanizing the social and economic situation. Whenever there is a question of actions clearly linked to this objective, we should try to carry them out as co-operatively as we can. We must never, nor must the unions, lose sight of the fact that our deadlines are no more identical than our means; that their approach remains essentially one of protest while ours is essentially one of persuasion, and above all, that union activity is most often limited and sectional while ours must of necessity be as broad in its reference as possible.

'Our party is and should remain open to all citizens who agree with these basics of our choice and action. There is room for many differences of opinion within this framework, and for all trends that respect the norms of decorum which no genuine democracy could do without. On condition that they not be petrified, but kept accessible to the human reality where they must stick or die, our structures should allow free discussion and free choice as well as the right of disagreement, providing this always be clearly dissociated from the official majority position of the party and that it not assume false airs of hard-line factionalism, which only sow more confusion in a society aspiring as never before to see things clearly.'

But despite the council's support of Lévesque, Robert Burns, the socialist labour lawyer who had been born below the CPR tracks, looked forward to the 1972 convention when he and other members of the left would attempt to move the party platform towards socialism.

One of the unanswered questions in the aftermath of October 1970 was the effect of the crisis on the Parti québécois. At the beginning of the year the party had financial problems, and membership had fallen from 80,000 to 30,000, a situation described by René Lévesque as normal for any party after the militancy of an election. The Chambly by-election on February 8 was widely regarded as an indicator of the effects of October, more particularly since the seat was vacated by the murder of Pierre Laporte. The Liberals ran Jean Cournoyer, who had joined the Bourassa cabinet, while the Péquistes stuck with Pierre Marois, the April 29 candidate. The campaign was a quiet, almost unnoticed, kitchen-and-parlour campaign. But both parties poured a lot of human resources into the Chambly kitchens. Unlike his actions in the general election Claude Ryan used *Le Devoir* to support the PQ. Realizing that a Liberal victory was certain, partly because Anglophones constituted 30 per cent of the population, Mr Ryan argued that a striking Liberal victory 'would lead the rest of the country to decide for the hundredth time that it was all over with the secessionist threat in Quebec and that they could sleep easy, sure of not being disturbed by a Liberal government committed to the present federalism and assured of Québécois support.' Such a conclusion would be dangerous, wrote Ryan, and the best way of stopping it would be for the voters 'to give M. Cournoyer a good fight.' A strong Péquiste showing, he concluded, would also give heart to the PQ, reveal that the voters did not associate it with the FLQ, and demonstrate that 'democracy is still alive in Quebec, and that the process of complete renewal of our political options, begun several months ago, is still going on.'

In the 1970 election 85 per cent of the voters had turned out, 48.5 per cent voting Liberal and 27.2 Péquiste. On February 8 only 66 per cent turned out with Cournoyer receiving 22,647 votes and Marois 11,452. 'Lévesque hailed the defeat as a victory 'which told all of Canada that political independence has not lost ground in these nine months, but gained it.'

Undoubtedly Chambly had helped the Parti québécois consolidate its position as a viable and legitimate political party. And as the Bourassa government faced one crisis after another – none of which strengthened its political appeal – and as neither the selection of Gabriel Loubier as the leader of the Union nationale nor its change of name to Unité-Québec promised miraculously to enhance its popularity, the PQ undoubtedly emerged as the most serious threat to the Liberals at the next election.

1972

Quiet times

By 1972 the Canadian voters had lost any illusions that Pierre Trudeau could walk on water and returned a minority government. The provinces too were disenchanted, and federal-provincial conferences revealed an emerging common front as all provinces complained of inadequate revenues, lack of planning and consultation, the threatened federal withdrawal from shared-cost programmes which would leave the provinces to face spiralling costs alone, and the increasing unreality of the taxing-spending equation. After a lengthy study a Senate-Commons committee recommended that there should be a new constitution 'based on functional considerations, which would lead to a greater decentralization of governmental powers in all areas touching culture and social policy and to a greater centralization in powers which have important economic effects at the national level.' At that very moment Claude Castonguay, Quebec's minister of social affairs, was fighting to the point of resignation for provincial primacy in the field of social policy and his colleague Jean-Paul L'Allier began his campaign for provincial control of communications. Premier Bourassa enunciated the goal of cultural sovereignty, while the Mouvement du Québec française escalated the campaign to make French the official language of Quebec and to force immigrant children to attend francophone schools.

Pierre Vallières gave himself up to police on January 24, spent a night in jail, and a week later was found working on a federal LIP project at Mont Laurier. The Bloc québécois surfaced on January 22, announced that it intended to field a slate of separatist candidates in the federal election, and sank. The Parti québécois published its manifesto, *Quand nous serons vraiment chez nous*, in April, but postponed until 1973 its annual congress because of the federal election campaign. René Lévesque's tour of France in June secured front-page coverage in Quebec newspapers, although in Brussels his assurance that the separation of Quebec was inevitable drew from Paul-Henri Spaak the dry comment that he did not believe 'in little independent states.'

René Lévesque obviously concluded that more was to be gained by running an anti-campaign during the federal election than by debating issues in a party convention. The Péquiste strategy was to keep the federal Liberals on the defensive by introducing a variety of separatist charges into the campaign, hoping to secure media coverage, build up its membership, and increase its support in the October 11 Quebec by-elections.

The campaign started on September 11 when Jacques Parizeau announced in Hull that the Trudeau government had a secret report which stated that a separatist Quebec was viable. The pattern was set when the Prime Minister felt compelled to admit the existence of the report, but denied the conclusions. A week later, the PQ declared that the Canadian army had a secret report on Quebec trade unions. When the army admitted it had a file, taken from newspapers, in case it had to quell civil disturbances, Lévesque was able to observe that the federal government regarded Quebec as an occupied territory. Patriation of the constitution, Quebeckers in the federal civil service, the costs of federalism – estimated at $200 million a year – the difference between Quebec's $13 million and Ontario's $200 million in federal research money, Ontario's higher standard of living, the imbalance between federal aid to western and Quebec agriculture, and a variety of other issues, were injected into the campaign. Finally, on October 16, Lévesque claimed that Liberals planned to stage violent incidents in Quebec to stampede the electorate. Winding up the anti-campaign on October 26, Lévesque stated that it had been a great success and had secured more than 25,000 new members.

The success was not evident in the October 11 by-elections. The Péquistes had high hopes for Duplessis where in 1970 the Liberals won the seat with 7,839 votes to the Péquistes' 5,612 and Union nationale's 3,310, and for some time there was speculation that Lévesque himself might run. Trade unions were strong in the riding's two

major centres, Sept-Iles and Schefferville, although it was questiona-
ble whether the support the PQ expected from the trade unions could
survive the equivocal position Lévesque adopted during the disturbances created by the common front in April. The PQ spent enormous
time and energy in the campaign, but the results were disillusioning, if
not shattering. With only the two parties running, the Liberals won
easily, 13,130 to 6,380. In Gatineau the PQ ran a poor third and, when
the by-election was replayed because of irregularities, decided not to
run at all.

However, the credibility of the party was increased by the acquisition of Claude Morin, who had resigned from the Quebec civil service
in 1971 expressing his dissatisfaction with the speed of constitutional
change and Trudeau's 'super-legalism,' which he felt was advancing
the cause of Quebec separatism. There was little doubt that Morin
would ultimately join the Péquistes, and virtually none after a March
11 speech in which he stated that 'Ottawa has a double objective: that
of making the Québécois ever more dependent on the federal St Vincent de Paul, and that of using a variety of precedents to obtain direct
or indirect control in new initiatives and areas of activity that are important in terms of the future.' Asked by a reporter why he did not join
Lévesque, Morin replied that he needed time to study carefully all the
alternatives.

Yet the conclusion was implicit in his *Le Pouvoir Québécois*, published early in May. A critical review of ten years in federal-provincial
relations, it argued that Quebec lost badly on almost every front. It
was no surprise when on May 21 he announced his affiliation with the
PQ. In a lengthy statement (*Le Devoir*, May 23) he explained his decision:

'I have made the decision to join the Parti québécois. The move,
which I intend to be as straightforward and calm as possible, marks
the culmination for me of a lengthy and sometimes wearing personal
development.

'It has been my lot for some years to be at the centre of Quebec-Ottawa discussions. My experience there has been a unique and stimu-
lating one. I have become acquainted with virtually every type of negotiation and political situation.

'Like so many others whose sincerity is as great as I believe my own
to be, I have spent years in hope. I have hoped that Quebec would ultimately find its place and feel comfortable within the present federal
structure. I have hoped stubbornly, deeply determined as I have been

to prove it still possible under our system for Quebec to take over its own destiny.

'But my hopes were deceived. The day came when I had to resign myself to a reckoning. No definite conclusion can be drawn from a single success or a single failure. However, after a number of years and four prime ministers, after experiencing all sorts of federalisms, "co-operative," "decentralized," "profitable," and so forth, I think at least one thing is obvious: never, under our present political system, can Quebec be truly itself. Ottawa is barely willing to let us operate a province under supervision, whereas in fact the Québécois are trying to build themselves a country. These two ambitions, Ottawa's and the Québécois', both consistent, both natural, are ultimately irreconcilable.

'I have observed something else. The inevitable tendency of the present federal system is to erode the power of Quebec. This is the will of the system far more than of the men in it. We are already well on our way down a path from which the Quebec government – gradually, and despite the periodic spasms of a kind of political death-agony – will emerge as an administrative outpost of the federal power.

'Once and for all, we must stop thinking that the federal government, any federal government, will eventually resign itself to the presence of a strong, dynamic government in Quebec. It is an impossibility under the present system. Since Confederation began, it has been Ottawa's aim to push all the buttons of any significance. I don't blame it for this. But let us remember that in order to achieve this aim, one that is quite understandable from the federal viewpoint, it is essential for Ottawa to stifle any impulse towards resistance on Quebec's part. Seconded by the other provinces, supported by an English-speaking population almost three times greater than our own, and seizing on any and all pretexts it desires, the federal power will always find a way of gobbling up Quebec's power, or whatever remains of it. And as time goes by, and the fields of government responsiblity increase, the differences between Ottawa and Quebec will become more and more serious and bring ever more frequent and generalized friction, confrontation, and conflict. We might be lost in a federal-provincial guerrilla war featuring an all-out attempt to exhaust us.

'In other words, what is now at stake is the very existence of an effective Quebec state capable of solving our problems, the very existence of the only political entity we can truly control and employ. In short, today's menace weighs against precisely that which is, for the

moment, our collectivity's sole significant means of action. And beyond all this, the challenge reaches us personally, as Québécois.

'But there is more. We have a whole society to organize. It is this society that must do the job and no outsider. Not only must it free itself
from its old complexes, but it must prepare to realize its potential as
well. Moreover, these must be done in a state of full awareness.

'Our Quebec society is neither more complex nor simpler than any
other. It aspires to be a normal society in which the workers can work,
the students study, and the government can govern.

'A society with clear, coherent and accepted social and economic
objectives and the appropriate tools for implementing them. A society,
certainly, that will put an end to the terrible waste of individuals, energies and resources that occurs under the present federal system, but
which will also assume the risks of its own destiny.

'For what the Parti québécois proposes is that we be an adult people, and no longer a cosseted, supervised tribal group headed for
complacent submission, painless assimilation, or political dependence. In short, the Parti québécois holds out the toughest solution:
being our own masters.

'Personally, my feelings in taking up this immense challenge are a
mixture of fear and joy. There are joys that are curiously heavy. Yet I
see it as my duty, in my own way, with my own ideas, to make my con-
tribution to the building of the Quebec we all want. And to do so openly, using the basic democratic right, mine as a citizen, to choose my
side ... '

The PQ was the most dynamic and creative, and the most valuable
institution for the economic, social, and political progress of Quebeckers, Morin argued. He joined the party, he concluded, because
'as a Québécois, I have no alternative ... The way offered us by the
Parti québécois is not the easy way – far from it – but it is the way of
dignity.'

1973

1973. James Bay
p. 122

Strike two: the election of October 29

Canada seemed about to enter the period of harmonic federalism as
the throne speech announced that Mr Trudeau would meet with the
provincial premiers 'to plan further steps in the harmonization of
goals, policies and programmes ...' The harmony could be heard
when Marc Lalonde conceded to Claude Castonguay in his battle for
an integrated provincially controlled social policy, but there was only
discord as L'Allier pressed for control over communications as an essential instrument of cultural sovereignty. The Gendron Commission
on the French language reported in February, but Premier Bourassa
resisted all the nationalist pressures for a new language policy before
the election although the direction the new policy would have to take
was clear. Meanwhile in Ottawa concern that the near defeat in 1972
was partly caused by opposition to the pace – if not the objective – of
bilingualism persuaded the Trudeau government to take its foot off
the accelerator.

For the second time in less than four years Quebec had the option of
voting against continued membership in the Canadian federal state.
When the results were in and the federalist option of the Liberals had
swept the province, Dennis Braithwaite exulted that 'you could say, if
you wanted to be mean, that Monday's election called Quebec's 100-
year-old bluff. I prefer to see it as a painful but sincere demonstration
by our French brothers that they are not fools and knaves first and
Canadians second, but Canadians first, last and always and I am
grateful to them for that.' There were, of course, other alternatives,

but the one explanation that could not be made to fit the facts was that Quebec had voted either for the idea of Canada or for the Canadian state as it existed. No party trumpeted the glory of being Canadian, or even of being part of Canada, for any purpose other than material and financial benefits. No party advocated anything other than continued decentralization to the point where the central government would be an economic shadow tolerated by members of the confederacy. Yvon Dupuis was an occasional exception when he led a Socred rally with 'O Canada.'

The Parti québécois

The initiative in the election was taken by the Parti québécois, and much of the campaign turned around its platform and the likely consequences of its success. The party had declined dramatically following the events of October 1970 and had been split badly during the labour unrest and violence a year later. But the *La Presse* demonstrations may have hastened the process of accommodation, for by the spring of 1972 the party could produce a draft manifesto for its October convention. According to Jacques Parizeau there had been no real differences between right and left or about means and ends within the party, simply questions of accent. He explained it all to his constituents, and *Le Devoir* (June 23) reported his thinking:

'We are getting ready to be the next government of Quebec, and this being the case, we should keep up our dialogue with the unions. Often this dialogue goes well – since fundamentally we are one on the aims and the basics – but sometimes we find ourselves telling the unions: no, there we do not agree. And they must not think in union circles, any more than we should in Parti québécois circles, that we will always agree on everything. And this is perfectly natural.

'M. Parizeau moved on to the main debate between the two tendencies in confrontation inside the PQ, giving this explanation:

'Clearly, our approach moved us to say, on one hand: we must get control of the economic decision centres in this country, and until we have regained control of the main decision centres we will be nowhere; our governments will simply reflect an outside power. This is what has been called the thesis of independentism.

'There is, M. Parizeau went on, another group in the Parti québécois that has said: that's true, but the issue is not the transfer of power from the small group who have it now to another small group who will typically speak French instead of English. Before we become independentists, they told us, we want to know how the transfer of power is going to work and who is going to get it.

'Basically, M. Parizeau said, these are differences in emphasis. Because those who want to alter the nature of the power are well aware that before it can be changed it has to be recovered. And on the other hand, those who want the recovery of power in order to achieve independence are well aware that the society must be changed as well.

'These are important differences in emphasis that have dominated the main debate in the party for two years – two years and a half – and eventually produced the platform you now have, as approved at the February convention.'

Michel Roy added that the architects of the seemingly impossible were Pierre Marois and Guy Joron, with some assistance from Camille Laurin. René Lévesque was persuaded to explore avenues that he had previously rejected and to delegate more responsibility, while M. Parizeau was encouraged to take a more sympathetic attitude towards the radicals and the trade union leaders.

Certainly the draft programme, *Quand nous serons vraiment chez nous*, had moved more explicitly to the left. The swing was apparent in the sections on economic planning, foreign ownership, financial institutions, and social policy. A section called 'La Socialisation en marche,' left out of the approved programme later, suggested that burial services, housing, television, holiday villages, and all insurance be state-provided. Trade unions would be extended to cover all workers, rather than the 40 per cent now unionized, and the unions would be one of the three 'interlocutoires' to put the new economic plan into effect. The draft also proposed direct worker participation in management but admitted that 'le grand problème est de savoir comment.' (A group at the February 1973 convention knew how, and, while Lévesque and other leaders were busy with the press, secured the passage of a resolution by the plenary session compelling industry in an independent Quebec to turn over power to workers' soviets. An embarrassed Lévesque persuaded the convention to rescind the motion, to the annoyance of at least one party member who ripped up his card in protest.)

While *Quand nous serons vraiment chez nous* promised that 'it is collectively, then, with the mass influx of all the most representative elements of the population, that the Plan's maturing will allow us to open the way to a democratic economy, to ever more aware participation by citizens in the orientation of the system and the complex decisions this requires,' a later section underlined 'The necessity of gradualism': 'What emerges from all this is the necessity of our using every means we can, working vigorously but with extreme care, to settle the very real and worsening conflict between people and the economic structures on which they depend. This conflict is as serious and infinitely harder to resolve than the one between people and political institutions. In both cases the point is to redefine, in order to better distribute, a power whose traditional concentration fails to reflect society's development. But the political plane is usually familiar to us, and all that is needed to reform it is a truly democratic government; on the other hand, the economic realm seems complex and disturbing, hostile particularly to those general theories which we are tempted by its very difficulty to substitute for the thoughtful and persistent action that is the only route to success.

'Thus, in a world where a goodly number of experiments have been tried and are widely known, it is obvious that doctrinaire socialism and suffocating state hegemony have not managed, any more than grandfather's capitalism in its various modes, primitive or refurbished, as practised up to now, to bring into being a paradise on earth or even decently to eliminate the most unjust abuses and inequalities.

'A project as noble and intelligent as participation deserves better than this, better than the delusions of revolutionary change that end in fraud no less cruel than that perpetrated by unbridled, unscrupulous "free enterprise." If we are going to change our economic life we must start with the most authentic resources at our command, and proceed with modesty and the appropriate gradualism as we alter the delicate mechanisms on which all our people depend for their daily bread.'

The Péquistes postponed their convention to run their federal anticampaign in October 1972. Their limited success and the outright failure in the provincial by-elections in the fall of 1972 apparently left the party disheartened and suffering from what Dominique Clift called 'a serious crisis of self-confidence as the result of finding itself becalmed on the political scene. The assurance and enthusiasm that were characteristic of the 1970 provincial elections have practically given out; instead, there are gloomy preoccupations over ideology, objectives and tactics. All this points to despondency about the party's prospects in the next provincial elections which are expected to take place in the spring of 1974' (*Montreal Star*, January 25). While

Clift may have been accurate in his impressions, the party had 62,400
members in the spring of 1973, twelve thousand more than in April
1970, and neither the February convention nor the spring fund-raising
suggested a party on the ropes.

The February 23-5 convention in Montreal was concerned with
drafting a party platform, and the twelve hundred delegates spent
much of their time discussing economic policy. Moderates easily defeated the radicals for control of the party executive, and much of the
radical philosophy of *Quand nous serons* was removed, although the
economic programme of the party remained far to the left of anything
proposed by the national or provincial New Democratic parties. As
outlined in the official platform, *Un gouvernement du Parti québécois
s'engage* ... the economic plan called for total national, regional, and
sectoral economic planning, and included abolition of finance companies, strict controls over financial institutions, nationalization of companies such as the Canadian Pacific (but not Bell), rigid controls on
foreign investment and foreign-owned companies, and a vastly expanded role for public corporations. Social policy in an independent
Quebec was to be based on a 'just' division of wealth and the complete abolition of poverty, at the root of which was a guaranteed annual income of $3,500, plus $500 a child and extensions of all forms of
financed health care, education, and housing.

In his opening address, René Lévesque had reiterated his belief
that the treatment of minorities was a measure of civilization. French
was declared to be the sole official and working language of the new
nation. The convention adhered to his position in retaining English
schools, but freezing the number of places at the time of independence unless the population diminished, in which case the number of
places in anglophone schools would also decline. Immigrants would
be educated exclusively in French schools and would have to pass a
French-language exam to qualify for a permanent visa or citizenship.

The party also attempted, it appears, to end the ambiguity concerning the actual acquisition of independence. The convention approved
the following statement:

'Therefore a Parti québécois government is committed to:

1. Immediate impetus for the movement towards sovereignty as
soon as this is proclaimed by the National Assembly – the transfer of
powers and jurisdiction might stretch over several months – while opposing any federal interference, even in the form of a referendum, this
being contrary to the right of peoples to self-determination.

2.   Holding a referendum, in order to solidify this independence, for the adoption of a constitution worked out with citizen participation at the riding level by delegates meeting in a constituent assembly.

3.   Reaching agreement with Canada on, among other things, the division of assets and liabilities and the ownership of public works, in conformity with international law and established practice.

4.   Requesting admission of Quebec to the United Nations and securing recognition from other states.

5.   Respecting those treaties binding Canada that are favourable to Quebec and, in denouncing other treaties, adhering to the rules of international law.

6.   Reaffirming and defending Quebec's inalienable rights over all its territory, including Labrador and the offshore islands of Nouveau-Québec; claiming possession of the Arctic lands and islands, now Canadian, which are its due by the same right as other northern countries; failing agreement on this subject, carrying out acts of judicial occupation (concession grants, founding of institutions, etc.) and taking the case before the International Court of Justice.'

Closing the convention, Lévesque stated that 'Not only would we have the right to bring about independence, we would have the duty to do it in order and clarity while staying in constant contact with the citizens. And this would mean that consultation would be indispensable in the constitution of the political system we propose. Yes or No?' The delegates screamed 'Yes!' Despite the attempt to clarify the procedure, it remained ambiguous and became increasingly so as the election campaign progressed.

The campaign really began before Premier Bourassa announced the election on September 25. During the spring Péquistes undertook an active fund-raising campaign and wound up with a giant rally at Quebec City on May 19. While the news event of the night was Lévesque's announcement that an election bank roll of $800,000 had been raised, the excitement was caused when Geneviève Bujold, the lithe star of *Kamouraska*, announced that she had become a Péquiste and planted kisses on the cheeks of the twenty-three regional fund-raisers. During the summer, the PQ worked subliminally, plastering the province with 'J'ai la goût du Québec' ('I have the taste of Quebec') posters.

The real campaign was opened by Lévesque at a downtown Montreal hotel on September 26. The 1973 Lévesque was cool; the campaign picture was softened in the forehead, the eyes, and the mouth, and portrayed a Lévesque ten years younger. Yet his style, though softer, retained the wit, the irony, and occasionally the savagery of the old Lévesque. A PQ victory, he said, would be 'a mandate to clarify everything that has been hidden from Quebeckers concerning the feasibility of independence and then to implant sovereignty through constitutional procedures based on a referendum,' a process he visualized as taking two years. The Liberals, he told one hundred generally sympathetic reporters, were 'minor leaguers who took signals from the bosses in Ottawa'; the Union nationale was 'an election fund in search of a party'; and the Créditistes were 'nice guys who had had their party stolen from them.' In his first and subsequent speeches M. Lévesque kept pulling out parts of the platform, anticipating piece-by-piece the promised budget for an independent Quebec, mocking the Liberals for their scare tactics and attacks on trade unions, and reiterating that independence represented not an economic gamble but a certain gain – imagine, (he told an audience in the depressed Gaspé) defence savings alone would build five hundred miles of four-lane highways a year.

The campaign was largely René Lévesque. The tactics were to move the leader and members of his team into a regional centre and secure massive press coverage and then to disperse them throughout the region for the rest of the day. The press, at least, gave little coverage to local candidates or to any spokesmen but Lévesque and, to a much lesser extent, Parizeau and Morin. The press, which certainly gave Lévesque as much copy and often better copy than Bourassa and the Liberals, did feature the additions to the Péquiste ranks: Abbé Louis O'Neill, who ran in Mercier; Yves Michaud, former Liberal MNA, who gave up his $30,000 a year travelling public relations job with the Quebec government to run in Bourassa; Antonio Flamand, a former Union nationale deputy, who ran in Rouyn-Noranda; Dr Robert Lussier, former minister of municipal affairs; and the sons of both Daniel Johnson and Jacques Bertrand. After the election there was some criticism of the strategy and tactics employed and of the central role played by the party executive and René Lévesque. While André Larocque represented the far left of the party, his view that the loss was partly attributable to an unrealistic strategy, conceived by the Montreal intellectuals and totally unrelated to conditions in the constituencies and to the 'presidential campaign' mapped out for Lévesque was shared by others. La Presse reported (December 3):

'Everything was organized around René Lévesque as if he was going to be the next prime minister of the province. The publicity committee wanted to set up a power strategy and in some respects had neglected the strategic ridings. They set off with the notion of getting sixty ridings – that is, gaining power – and on that basis scratched out some theories. However, a week before the election it was realized that the Créditistes no longer existed from the voting standpoint. Unfortunately the image they had chosen to go with their aims was much too big, and it was too late to recover any ridings.'

The Péquiste budget

If the outcome of the election was influenced by the campaign or by argument, the Parti québécois budget was a crucial statement. Lévesque had promised the budget at the beginning of the campaign, but it was not revealed until October 9 at a Quebec City press conference. Both the budget and the conference were designed to give the appearance of a real budget, a budget as likely to be implemented as anything Raymond Garneau might present in the Assembly and accompanied by carefully prepared press releases as easy for the press to feed into print. Introducing the budget for 1975-6, M. Parizeau stated that it was the financial statement to accompany the 1973 platform, as detailed as any official budget and proof of the technical competence of the Parti québécois to govern. The budget was based on the 1973-4 provincial and federal budgets and was projected with appropriate provision for an increased volume of services, increased prices (4 per cent), and increased civil service salaries (7 per cent). It proved beyond question, said Lévesque and Parizeau, that an independent Quebec was financially viable. PQ Finance Minister Parizeau's lengthy statement first sought to assure the electorate that the budget was based on full recovery of federal taxes in Quebec and full payments of all federal payments. He then explained the process of negotiation that would have to precede the first budget for the new state in 1975-76:

'This budget bears a date. It is the budget for the fiscal year 1975-6. Supposing that the Parti québécois were called to form the government on October 29, Quebec's independence would obviously not be achieved on the 30th. The assets of the federal government would have to be divided up: the operation would apply equally to post offices and railways as to gold and foreign exchange reserves and much more. We would have to divide up the federal public debt, since a portion of that debt was incurred for the Québécois. We will have to provide for the Quebec incorporation of companies that have hitherto been Canadian. These Quebec companies will have to adhere to rules laid down by the Foreign Investment Code to identify those sectors where foreign control is permissible and those calling for a majority Québécois interest.

'We will have to prepare to set up a Quebec central bank, a ministry of foreign affairs, and other bodies required by an independent state. We will also have to prepare for a customs union with Canada, so that the movement of goods between the two countries can continue smoothly. This is so important for both countries that we foresee no major difficulty except, perhaps, with agricultural products.

'We will also have to investigate the possibility of establishing a common currency between the two countries. At a time when the idea of such common currencies is under examination by modern industrial states, it would be absurd for a Quebec government not to consider it in preparation for independence. However, the question remains much more difficult than that of the customs union. Each of the two countries involved could lay down conditions unacceptable to the other.

'Quebec must then be ready to issue its own money, that is to follow the usual, customary, and conventional course of countries becoming independent.

'We must also prepare for Quebec's entry into international bodies.

'Finally, we must prepare a draft political constitution for an independent Quebec and have it ratified by referendum.

'It is only when these steps have been taken that Quebec becomes independent.'

Surprisingly, the PQ finance minister expected that almost all the programmes outlined in the party platform could be introduced in year one of independence without an increase in taxes, partly as a result of the economies of a single administration and the greater efficiency of some programmes and partly as a result of a 9.5 per cent increase in gross national product.

'At this level a tax volume is still being generated, taking into account the planned fiscal reforms, which, together with an absolutely reasonable rate of borrowing, enables the Quebec state to make substantial improvements in the social security system as well as to undertake and finance a major reorganization of the Quebec economy, without having to rely on those putative Messiahs, the foreign financiers. Not that an independent Quebec rejects all foreign capital input: that would be childish as well as ridiculous. We must, however, be in a position to see the foreigner as a contributor and no more.

'This general view of the economy prompts us to earmark substantial sums for regaining Quebec control in some major economic institutions, making massive investments in long-neglected sectors, and securing company mergers to improve ability to meet international competition.

'Money attracts money. The more Quebec can find the materials for its development at home, the more easily will it attract foreign capital. The traditional attitude of only looking outside to finance major Quebec projects is an expression, in a country that is industrial, developed, and collectively quite rich, of the colonialist reactions represented by our traditional political leaders.

'It will undoubtedly be maintained among traditional leaders that independence means the flight of foreign capital and thus a slowdown in Quebec's growth rate. Is it necessary' to remind them once again that Coca-Cola's chief adversary is not the Parti québécois but Pepsi-Cola; that General Electric's main enemy is not the Parti québécois but Westinghouse; that Sun Life's main enemy is not the Parti québécois but the Prudential?

'Big companies compete with one another. None will withdraw from a market unless obliged to. We have no intention of reaching that point. The combination of this competition with the investments we have the will and means to make ourselves – these are the best safeguards for our prosperity.'

Government borrowing was estimated at $900 million, marginally less than the billion borrowed for Quebec by the federal and provincial governments in 1973-4.

M. Parizeau then turned to the value of 'le dollar québécois': 'This immediately raises the problem of the influence of the Quebec dollar's value on the budget. It is a false problem, as all the technical people are aware. We have never seen the Finance Minister of Canada set his budget with the announcement that the Canadian dollar would be worth $1.05 American or 95 cents.

'Since all the information we have indicates that the present governments' main line of defence is going to be to try to muddy debate on the budget with discussion of exchange rates, we must reply before the muddying occurs. This information is reliable, and it must be admitted that for the past three years the information the Parti

The Renébuck

Montreal *Gazette*, October 23, 1973

québécois has produced on the federal government and the provincial government has usually been sound and solidly backed up.

'Cabinet Minister Pierre Laporte commented in the course of the 1970 election campaign that a Quebec dollar would be worth 65 cents. In the current election campaign, Cabinet Minister St Pierre has put its value at 75 cents. And the document on Quebec independence prepared by Prime Minister Trudeau's office at the time of the October, 1972, federal election put it at 85 cents.

'We must stop this progression before it reaches $1.05 or $1.10. When a country has an unemployment rate as high as Quebec's, it has no interest in an inflated exchange rate; quite the reverse.

'The fact is that, as with all other currencies, the value of the Quebec dollar is going to be determined by the state of Quebec's balance of payments. On the foreign exchange markets, the Quebec dollar is going to float like the Canadian dollar, the pound sterling, the German mark, the French franc ...

'A surprising result, but technically incontrovertible and valid for all countries. The Quebec budget will be all the easier to administer if the Quebec dollar does not have too high a value in relation to the Canadian dollar and the American dollar. A Quebec dollar worth 95 cents of a Canadian dollar would be ideal at the present time. At $1.05 it would lead to more unemployment than we have now. We can do without that! In fact we will move around like the Canadian dollar in relation to the American, sometimes below, sometimes above in relation to an American dollar.'

A shortened version of the full budget was printed for popular distribution. On the expenditure side the shortened version neglected to point out that loans of almost $500 million to a variety of state agencies brought the expenditure to $11.9 million, but that was a small oversight. The reaction to the budget in Quebec was as serious as the budget presentation itself, and the press played it as if it were the national or provincial budget. Even in English Canada it secured substantial coverage in those newspapers that attempted to provide national coverage. While minor technical flaws amused some economists and reporters, the major question posed by both French and English observers was whether an independent Quebec could sustain a 9.5 per cent growth in GNP, or indeed any growth rate at all. Vincent Prince suggested that, despite the PQ's denial that it was hypothetical, 'it is founded, in fact, on the most optimistic possible hypothesis, assuming that independence will have absolutely no effect on the economic growth rate of Quebec.' Prince did not accept the hypothesis (*La Presse*, October 11). Nor did Claude Ryan, who wrote on October 16 that to recall the uncertainty and declined economic activity after Expo 67 was to demonstrate, not 'timidity,' but a good memory. French Canadian papers also wondered whether English Canada would be the gentle negotiators of the division of the country. It remained for the *Globe and Mail* (October 25) among the more responsible papers in the country to suggest that Canada might not be an easy negotiator of a common currency or customs union and that in open competition there could be considerable damage since Canada absorbed 68 per cent of Quebec exports and 30 per cent of its total product.

Another major question leading to the continued battle of the documents on the Quebec-Ottawa trade offs was the accuracy of the Parti québécois figures on federal taxing and spending in Quebec. On October 23 the PQ released two tables prepared by the Ministry of Industry and Commerce and leaked to the PQ. The first purported to show that between 1947 and 1971 Quebec had exported $10.7 billion in capital, while the second asserted that between 1961 and 1971 the federal government raised $2,616 million in taxes more than it spent in Quebec. Industry Minister Guy Saint-Pierre admitted that the tables were authentic but added that the PQ had omitted the accompanying explanatory text and that the tables were in conflict with another set of statistics. Pending a reconciliation of this contradiction, he had decided not to release them. On October 24 Finance Minister Garneau issued a lengthy statement and a further set of figures which seemed to admit that, in the early 60s at least, Quebec was a net loser on the statistical tradeoff but that by 1971-2 Quebec reaped a rich harvest in both benefits and cash flows from Canadian federalism. A simplified version of his figures is shown in the table below.

Federal taxing and spending in Quebec (millions of dollars)

	1963–4	1967–8	1971–2
Cash flow			
Federal Taxes	2,014.1	2,739.2	4,070.6
Cash expenditure	1,788.4	2,689.3	4,460.8
Balance	−225.7	−90.5	+390.2
Benefits	1,949.6	2,855.9	4,732.7
Balance	−64.5	+116.7	+653.1

The PQ believed it had a major issue, however, and on October 26 bought full-page ads reading: 'IN THE PAST 24 YEARS QUEBEC HAS OFFERED ITSELF THE LUXURY OF EXPORTING 10 BILLION 700 MILLION DOLLARS THAT HAVE AIDED THE DEVELOPMENT OF OTHERS.

A final issue generated by the PQ campaign was nothing less than the exact significance of a vote for the party. The ambiguity persisted as to the meaning of an electoral victory, but during the campaign it became increasingly clear that the PQ wanted the electorate to believe that a vote for them was not a vote for independence. In Quebec City and Chicoutimi on October 17-18, for example, René Lévesque observed that it had taken two referendums before Newfoundland entered confederation. Claude Beauchamp attempted to explain what he called the new 'nuances' of the PQ in *La Presse* (October 9):

'It's not entirely election strategy, a desire not to frighten people, that has prompted the Parti québécois to play down the idea of independence from the outset of the campaign.

'This year brings us important elements that were not in the PQ platform or public statements of 1970.

'The political commitment of Claude Morin, that former senior civil servant of the Quebec government specializing in federal-provincial and international relations, and his arrival in the trenches are not unrelated to the new accents of the PQ.

'As the campaign opened, M. Morin asserted frankly that Quebec's independence, or more precisely, political sovereignty, would not occur without a referendum, without fresh consultation of the québécois citizenry.

'This was not an isolated voice. The PQ returns − has returned − to the two-part expression of the very beginning of René Lévesque's movement: sovereignty-association.

'However this return to the sources does sow a certain confusion here and there.

'Thus, a PQ newcomer, Yves Michaud, also formerly a senior civil servant and now a candidate in Bourassa, has described himself in an open-line programme on CKVL as an "Orthodox federalist," that is, hoping for a "new pact," a "new understanding" with the rest of Canada.

'What exactly are we dealing with?

'Undoubtedly the answer must be sought in the remarks of the party leader. In each of his speeches, Mr Lévesque devotes twenty minutes or so to explaining the process by which independence is to be achieved.'

Confusion continued to remain, if not reign, 'here and there,' but the Parti québécois attempted to put it to rest in a full-page ad on October 26 ('What will happen the next day?'). A day later, the last day, another full-page ad ('Aujourd'hui', reprinted here) removed any ambiguity. But it did not seem quite the position that had been agreed to in February.

Apparently the tactic worked. Mark Wilson (*Montreal Star*, October 23) interviewed a Matapedia farmer who admitted he was working for the PQ because of their economic and social platform and their belief in the dignity of the individual and 'standing on our own feet.' Asked if he was not worried about the consequences of independence, he replied: 'Less than last time, I think. Besides, electing the PQ doesn't necessarily mean independence, you know, there would be a referendum. It's a way of improving a bargaining position, like taking a strike vote. There's got to be some changes.'

René Lévesque had some very powerful allies. While the leaders of the three major trade unions were displeased with many of the positions taken by the moderates in the PQ, they made their position unequivocally clear. Following their release from jail on May 16, Laberge, Pepin, and Charbonneau stated that they were going to implement plans to form 'Popular Political Action Committees' to defeat the Bourassa government. The leaders had to be cautious not only because of internal divisions but also because the PQ itself had no desire to be openly embraced by the militant trade union leaders.

The most cautious was the CNTU (Confederation of National Trade Unions/Confédération des syndicats nationaux), whose 1972 convention resolution favouring increased militancy had been left largely ineffective. But before the election it printed fifty thousand pamphlets delineating its lack of enthusiasm for the Liberals and leaving little option but support for the PQ. At its planning session on September 26, the FTQ (Fédération des travailleurs du Québec) avoided taking an official position but asserted that the Bourassa government was the worst anti-syndicalist government in Quebec's history. Louis Laberge went further and called on the FTQ membership to overthrow the Liberals by supporting members sympathetic to the labour movement, most of whom, he added with a smile, might be campaigning under the PQ banner. By October 2, M. Laberge was quoted in *Le Devoir* as stating that the Liberals were not only irresponsible but even had strong fascist tendencies. André Laclerc, director of political action for the FTQ, estimated that 55 per cent of the 550 FTQ organizers were working for

Aujourd'hui,
je vote pour la seule équipe prête à former un vrai gouvernement.

En 1975,
par référendum, je déciderai de l'avenir du Québec.

Une chose à la fois! Chaque chose en son temps.

 **Je vote Parti Québécois.
Je vote pour le vrai!**

the Parti québécois. Yvon Charbonneau, leader of the CEQ (Corporation des enseignants du Québec), made his anti-Bourassa and pro-Péquiste sympathies clear and unsuccessfully tried to secure a united front. At the July convention of the CEQ, 603 of the two thousand delegates filled out a questionnaire, of whom 54 per cent favoured independence, 42.5 per cent with association with Canada and 11.6 per cent without; 10 per cent were satisfied with the federal system; 23.9 per cent advocated greater decentralization and 3.3 per cent more centralization; and 2.5 per cent favoured annexation to the United States.

Firmly behind the Parti québécois was also the Mouvement Québec Français. In mid-October the MQF released a pamphlet *Je vote pour un Québec français*, outlining the language policies of the four parties, and Francois-Albert Angers stated on October 18 that the 750,000 members of the eight organizations that made up the MQF had no other choice but to vote for the PQ and independence.

If the nationalist and unionist leadership carried the membership the PQ threatened to be extremely strong in urban francophone Quebec.

Third parties

From the outset it seemed clear that the election would be a two-party fight. Both the Parti québécois and the Liberals wished to see the electorate polarized, and the minor parties found it difficult to determine who to attack or how to get their own platform and identity established. On the whole, both the Union nationale and the Créditistes took up positions to the right of the Liberals and the PQ, explicitly or implicity adopted a posture that stopped short of, though was prepared to consider, separatism, and divided their time between attacks on the government and the Péquistes.

Amid cries of 'Vive l'Union nationale' on January 14 Unité Québec disappeared and the Union nationale re-emerged. Gabriel Loubier told the convention that the UN must return to its roots and form a new alliance of nationalists, Liberals, and Conservatives to represent once again 'the union of the vital forces in the nation.' Anticipating policy positions to be adopted later, Loubier denounced the Bourassa government as the 'puppet of the federal government,' described the Canadian constitution as a dead letter, and called for a new constitution. The form the new constitution would take became clear on March 4 when M. Loubier spoke to two thousand party members at a Montreal fund-raising dinner. The party stood firmly behind Souveraineté association, a new federal system based on ten sovereign provinces who would negotiate their mode of association and the powers they would give to the central government.

While the Union nationale was visibly disintegrating, the Créditistes appeared to take on new life. In 1970 they had secured 11 per cent of the popular vote and a dozen seats, but with the demise of the Union nationale and the election of the dynamic Yvon Dupuis as their new leader, many observers believed that the party threatened to become an important factor in Quebec politics.

Apart from the platform, and the appeal to law and order and all varieties of discontent, M. Dupuis rellied heavily on his personal style – the mockery, the irony, the personal assaults, and the appeal to the prejudice of his audience. He was merciless in his attacks on his opponents, mocking Loubier, describing Bourassa as 'Bou Bou, the prefabricated man,' and particularly castigating Lévesque. Separatists were like terrorists, he told seven thousand people in Montreal on October 21, and 'you can't build a Quebec on hate, violence, and the October events ... It isn't by telling our children that guys like Jacques Rose and Paul Rose are models of virtue when we all know that they are terrorists whom we vomit from our mouths from the four corners of Quebec.' In his attacks on the PQ he was joined by an enthusiastic Réal Caouette who helped kick off the Créditiste campaign in Quebec city on October 8. 'I will not appeal to hate or disunity but to the brotherhood of Quebeckers. It will be a campaign of love ... You can tell a man by the company he keeps. M. Lévesque, leader of the Parti québécois, is a fine man they say but look around him at the union leaders, the revolutionaries. It's about time Quebec stopped following other countries into socialism. If the separatists gain power we know Quebec will experience the same disorder that Chile is experiencing today.'

Throughout the campaign there remained some concern in both Liberal and PQ camps about the likely effect of the Créditistes, particularly in Montreal and some rural areas formerly won by the Union nationale. On the whole, however, it had become clear early in the campaign that Dupuis was not going to make the inroads in Montreal that he had built his strategy around and that he might find it difficult to hold his own even in traditional Créditiste strongholds.

Bourassa builds

There had been speculation all summer that Bourassa would call a fall election, although many observers agreed with him on August 14 when he stated that he could see no good reason for having a general election. Speculation increased following the Mount Orford meeting of leading Liberals late in August, for Bourassa's speech certainly outlined the economic, social, and cultural themes of an election campaign. The Liberal caucus apparently considered an election on September 13 (Montreal *Gazette*) with the veteran Gaspé campaigner Bona Arsenault swinging rural support for an early election against the wishes of four senior cabinet ministers who either wanted more time to create jobs (Saint-Pierre), another budget without a tax increase (Garneau), a firm language policy (L'Allier), which apparently drew from Bourassa the statement that a firm language policy would have to come after an election, or believed there were no burning issues to justify an election (Cournoyer). In all probability Bourassa had already decided on an election, and the cabinet changes announced on September 20 clearly anticipated one. Out were Pinard and Tremblay, both old war horses involved in charges of political favouritism, Claire Kirkland-Casgrain, who had earlier announced her retirement, and Claude Castonguay, whose appointment to the board of the Quebec Deposit and Investment Fund scotched the rumours that he was leaving in anger or disagreement.

There was much to be said for an election. The economy was booming, despite inflation and unemployment. Labour troubles were at a minimum, and the anti-Bourassa labour movement was more or less divided and impotent. There had been four budgets without increased taxes, and the government was able to announce the implementation, as of January 1974, of the new social security system based on a major increase in family allowances which had emerged from the federal-provincial miil as Claude Castonguay had wanted it. Not only did the new programme bring new money to most Quebeckers, but it was also used as proof of what Bourassa called 'un fédéralisme positif' (*Journal de Montréal*, September 25). Moreover, Bourassa could argue, as in his September 25 statement, that an election was necessary because the government had fulfilled its first mandate and was now ready to present 'a new plan of action,' that the electoral map had been redrawn and the National Assembly was therefore unrepresentative, and that the province could do without the uncertainty that always accompanied rumours of an election.

Yet, like all politicians, Bourassa went to the country because he believed he could win. Apparently the man behind the political strategy was Paul Desrochers, the quiet mastermind of Bourassa's Liberal party. Desrochers was a great believer in polls and commissioned a number throughout the year. In February the Liberals found that Dupuis and the Créditistes were moving, but major polls conducted in March, April, and July suggested that the Créditistes had peaked and were losing ground, while the PQ was holding steady at about 30 per cent of the vote. After the election, Desrochers told Richard Cléroux of the *Globe and Mail* (October 31) that questionnaires confirmed the Liberal view that economic questions were uppermost in the electorate's mind, while language was only an issue for 1.45 per cent of the respondents. Although Desrochers pressed for an early election, the results exceeded his expectations. He told Cleroux that the Liberals had fifty-seven sure ridings, and twenty-eight where the chances were better than 75 per cent. But he didn't expect to win more than eighty-five seats and believed that the Créditistes would get fifteen, the PQ eight, and the UN two – Loubier and Armand Russell would win because of their personal qualities.

The Liberal party built and centred its literature and campaign around Bourassa. The slogan for the election was Bourassa construit ('Bourassa builds'). Posters and foldouts featured Bourassa against a montage of hydro developments, booming factories, superhighways, happy young people and beaming children – 'Building Together a Better Quebec.' The platform was outlined in *A New Plan for Action*, a seventy-five-page booklet in which the Liberals reviewed their past performance and promised even more in the future: the use of Quebec savings in Quebec development by the issue of bonds which would be tax exempt, tax exemptions for the profits of small and medium-sized businesses which were reinvested in Quebec, tax exemptions for family allowances, tax exemptions for workers' tools, the new billion-dollar social security system, and new support for housing and controls on land speculation. On the political side the Liberals revealed a sensitivity to criticism by promising decentralization of educational administration, increased flexibility in educational budgeting, and greater access to the government and its bureaucracy.

While the Liberals promised 'on a priority basis ... to obtain a fiscal division which will enable Quebec to fully assume its constitutional responsibilities,' and repeatedly emphasized the importance of cultural reaffirmation, the platform was blunt in its support for federalism:

'Canadian unity is absolutely essential to the development of Qué-bec society and to the improvement of the quality of life of its citizens. *The option of the Liberal party of Québec is clear and specific; it is that of Canadian federalism.*

'Separatism must be rejected because it condemns Québec to tragic backlogs in terms of development and because it exposes Que-beckers, especially the most disadvantaged among them, to irremedi-able economic social harm ...

'*Unacceptable* in its economic and social consequences for Que-beckers, *separatism*, linked with monetary union, is consequently *perfectly useless* for Québec since it would lead, in fact, to a fictitious, illusory and ephemeral form of sovereignty, a sovereignty Quebeckers would have to find costly and which, in any event, they absolutely do not need. The Liberal team firmly believes in the possibility of building a modern, dynamic and creative Québec society while sharing with the rest of Canada *the total Canadian experience.*'

Liberal policy was based on two cornerstones: decentralized feder-alism and cultural sovereignty at the constitutional level and eco-nomic federalism in the area of federal-provincial relations. 'The idea of cultural sovereignty specifies the degree of freedom of action nec-essary for Quebec within Canada to provide itself, internally and ex-ternally, with the policies and programmes necessary to safeguard and develop the French language and culture,' the New Plan ex-plained. '*To wish to build a Quebec culturally sure of itself is not to deny Canada.* On the contrary, it is an effort to enrich the Canadian cultural personality with the dynamism and vitality of the French lan-guage and culture.' Once re-elected the Liberals intended 'to reopen the constitutional review file.'

The campaign itself was deceptively simple. The government rested on its record, and promised a continuation of economic growth, financial responsibility, and improved social security. There was enough profitable federalism and cultural reaffirmation or sover-eignty to keep the Quebec Firsters more or less content, enough law and order and social peace to prevent the Liberals from being too badly outflanked by the UN or the Créditistes, and enough doom and gloom about the economic consequences of separatism to frighten all but the suicidal. Initially, Bourassa played the law-and-order game reasonably heavily: 'No one will be above the law in Quebec,' or 'You were wrong, Mr Charbonneau, Mr Laberge, Mr Pepin, to think you were above the law,' he reiterated again and again. From the outset he also emphasized that the next stage of growth was the quality of life, based on a sound economy and the cultural development of the province. The announcement two days after the campaign started that the province would take over licensing control of cable television on November 1, two days after the election, was not coincidental. 'The regulations ... are only a first stage on the way to a recovery by Quebec of all the instruments of its cultural development, notably in the sector of communications,' read a statement prepared by Communications Minister L'Allier. And in Kenogami on October 2, Bourassa promised cultural independence in a revised constitution, which would also include expanded provincial control over taxation and social policy.

But the bulk of every speech was devoted to the economic consequences of separatism, particularly after the budget was released by the PQ on October 9. The premier had baited the PQ to bring it down so he could 'shoot it full of holes' and had retired for a few days to examine the budget in detail when it appeared. While the premier and his finance minister did poke holes in the budget – finding minor and major miscalculations and omissions – the Liberal response was really directed to the budget's assumptions that economic growth would continue after a PQ victory. The Liberals charged that the assumed 9.5 per cent increase in GNP was absurd, that capital investment would fall off, if not dry up, that the dollar would fall to 70 cents or below, that the cost of living would rise dramatically with a decline in the value of the dollar and the standard of living drop, that debt costs would soar, and that there would be a massive exodus of young people to escape unemployment and a low standard of living. Over three thousand young Quebeckers left the province during the economic uncertainty of 1969, Bourassa continually repeated, but in 1972 the numbers had fallen to less than half: 'As leader of the Liberal party, as head of the government of Quebec, I will not permit the young, the workers and the disadvantaged to pay the price.' Concluding his first major speech on the budget at Lachute on October 12, during which he described a budget that cut taxes, increased expenditures, and had a surplus as 'créditisme pour intellectuels,' he stated: 'Again, all these things, all these problems with the budget start with M. Parizeau's predictions, themselves evincing wild optimism in the midst of the best economic year in history. According to him, once independence is declared or announced things will be even better.

'What are we to take from this? In the days to come I will have occasion to point out the irresponsibility of the other parties as well. This PQ accounting exercise is the richest proof, the most meaningful evidence, the most conclusive demonstration that the real solution for the québécois is not the separation of Quebec. The real solution for the québécois is cultural sovereignty in an economic federation as offered by the Liberal party of Quebec.

'The fact of our French culture is the thing that sets us off from the rest of North America. Here is where our independence is to be won. Here is where our first efforts have been directed and where our focus will continue to be. Even though the federal government is unwilling, it will have to give way. This is a question of common sense, for an English-speaking majority cannot be allowed to control the cultural development of a French-speaking minority. Here, there can be no question of the Quebec government's abandoning its objective. Our policy is clear, definite and quite firm.

'Our Frenchness separates us from the rest of Canada. Yet in economic terms we are North Americans. Now the PQ's proposal, eloquently confirmed in its budget, quite simply amounts to throwing our future as a culture into jeopardy for the sake of an economic sovereignty that is an utter delusion.

'All the points have been studied: the monetary union, the Quebec currency, the temporary monetary union, and the fiscal product. We will return to the flaws in this budget.

'The choice of October 29 is more obvious than ever: if we want to keep on building Quebec, if we want to keep on entrenching the security of the Québécois, increasing the prosperity of the Québécois, our choice is more obvious than ever; it is the Liberal party of Quebec' (*Le Devoir*, October 16).

The Liberals seldom went quite as far as the other parties in distorting the issues or engaging in vicious attacks on the PQ. But one pamphlet, distributed at least in Montréal-Ste Marie, came close to being politics for the simple-minded:

LOSING your FAMILY ALLOWANCE and OLD-AGE PENSION cheques; AN INCREASE of at least 100% in INCOME TAX;
CAPITAL MOVING OUT, INVESTMENT HARD TO FIND, and the LOSS OF COUNTLESS JOBS:
Possible ENTRENCHMENT OF A SOCIALIST SYSTEM and control of consumer goods (RATIONING);
NATIONALIZATION of trade and industry and the disappearance of the personal enterprise of the citizen who will turn into JUST A NUMBER

The results

Polls conducted by the Centre de recherches sur l'opinion publique
(CROP) provided one picture of the mood of the Quebec electorate:

	PL	PQ	Créd.	UN	?
May 1972	42%	15%	8%	4%	31%
May 1973	33	20	13	3	31
October 1	37.8	18.8	9.6	4.6	28.4
October 18	35.2	21.1	9.8	4	25.3

Other polls during the campaign revealed much the same pattern. Including only those who had decided, all the polls taken during the
campaign gave the Liberals between 52 and 56 per cent, the PQ between 26 and 32, the Créditistes 8 to 14, and the Union nationale 4 to
6.

The October 1 telephone poll revealed that 36.4 per cent felt Bourassa was the best leader, to 18.7 for Lévesque; 57.1 per cent believed
that the Liberals would win; and 48.9 per cent were satisfied with the
government. The poll also indicated that the Liberals were running
25.9 per cent to 30 per cent for the PQ among francophone Montreal-
ers, where Lévesque also ran ahead of Bourassa 28 to 25 per cent. A
Le Devoir – Le Soleil poll released on October 20 stated that 56.6 per
cent of those polled were satisfied with the government, a figure remarkably close to the Liberal vote on October 29. Another poll indicated that 61.5 per cent believed that independence would lead to
economic deterioration, and 46.9 per cent that it would improve the
state of French language and culture.

In terms of the popular vote the polls were reasonably accurate, but
the number of seats won by the Liberals was at least a dozen more
than the PQ or the Liberals had estimated on the eve of the election
when it was clear that opinion had been successfully polarized. The
following table provides the details.

Unlike some elections, the results were not due to a hopelessly ar-
chaic distribution system or to extensive corruption. The election was
the first to be fought under redistribution approved in 1972, and although rural Quebec was still overrepresented, only eight ridings exceeded the forty thousand maximum and four the twenty-five thousand minimum. Greater Montreal had received nine more seats and
Quebec one, and the Assembly was increased from 108 to 110 seats

Popular vote, 1973 preliminary figures
(1970 results in parentheses)

	Vote	Percentage of votes	Seats
Lib.	1,623,734	54.8 (41.8)	102 (72)
PQ	897,809	30.3 (23)	6 (7)
PC	294,706	9.9 (11.1)	2 (12)
UN	146,209	4.9 (19.6)	0 (17)

while eight rural ridings disappeared. Although there were the usual charges that the election in some ridings had been stolen, the election appeared to be cleaner than most, and not even the PQ seriously believed that Liberal manipulations had beaten them.

The Péquistes increased their percentage of the popular vote in every riding except two of their strongholds in Montreal East. In twenty-four constituencies their vote increased more than 10 per cent, and they received over 40 per cent of the popular vote in twenty-six ridings, twenty-one of which were in Montreal. Yet in at least fifty seats there was no contest at all, as the Liberals polled more than twice the votes of their closest competitor. On the other hand, nine ridings were won by less than a thousand votes, and had the decision gone the other way, seven leading Péquistes would have been in the Assembly – René Lévesque, Claude Morin, Pierre Marois, Camille Laurin (the defeated house leader), Guy Joron, Gilles Proulx, and Guy Bisaillon. A switch of less than 10 per cent the other way, however, would have wiped out the entire Péquiste contingent. A regional breakdown, using preliminary official figures, is presented in the next table.

During the election René Lévesque had warned of the potentially explosive situation if the anglophone minority kept in power a party not supported by a majority of francophones, and both Loubier and Dupuis had appealed to English-speaking constituents for their support. After the election it seemed clear that while anglophone Quebec had overwhelmingly supported the Liberals, the Parti québécois had significantly increased its support among non-francophones. Lévesque estimated that his party had secured 6 per cent of the English vote, double that in 1970 (Montreal *Gazette*, November 9). *La Presse* polls (taken during and after the election but published November 19-24) suggested that about 30 per cent of low-income anglophone

Sober second thought

Halifax *Chronicle-Herald*, October 31, 1973

Popular vote by region

Region	Total Vote	% Lib	% PQ	% PC	% UN	Seats
Montreal Region	619,993	51.7	34.3	10.2	4.4	21
Montreal East	541,126	49.7	44.3	4.0	1.7	18
Montreal West	463,572	71.9	22.7	2.7	1.5	16
Quebec City	147,761	54.5	35.8	5.3	3.4	5
Quebec Region	283,055	53.1	21.5	16.5	9.0	11
Three Rivers	151,682	48.7	23.7	11.5	16.2	6
Eastern Townships	270,867	49.8	20.4	21.4	8.3	11
Ottawa Region	75,398	62.0	23.8	10.7	2.8	3
North West	83,939	49.0	16.4	31.2	3.0	4
Saguenay–Lac St Jean	178,809	48.3	38.0	6.9	6.0	7
Lower St Lawrence–Gaspé	151,777	54.1	26.3	13.4	6.1	8

workers and about 10 to 11 per cent of white-collar and high-income blue-collar workers supported the PQ outside of Montreal; in Montreal itself, there was no white-collar support for the Péquistes. Pierre Drouilly, in a lengthy and complicated analysis in the separatist daily *Le Jour* (February 28-March 5, 1974) published the breakdown for the Montreal region presented in the following table.

Popular vote in the Montreal region

		% PQ	% Lib	% PC-UN
West	francophones	47.1	44.1	8.8
	non-francophones	0.4	97.9	1.7
North	francophones	51.1	44.3	4.6
	non-francophones	5.3	93.6	1.1
South	francophones	53.2	41.3	5.5
	non-francophones	13.7	81.0	5.3
East	francophones	54.3	88.4	7.3
	non-francophones	43.7	80.0	8.3

On the whole, most observers agreed that in Montreal the two parties ran very close among the francophones, with the PQ having an edge in some sections of the city. For the province, polls suggested that the two parties were neck-and-neck among young francophones, and the Liberals (46 per cent) ahead of the PQ (38 per cent) and the PC-UN combined (16 per cent) among all francophones.

The question remained, as it had since René Lévesque created the Parti québécois, whether those who supported the party did so because of its constitutional position, its leader, or its ideology. Perhaps the most reliable response to the question was provided by the *La Presse* polls carried out by three Montreal academics during and after the election. One of their studies indicated that 49.7 per cent were favourable to federalism, 24 per cent unfavourable, and 26.3 per cent uncertain; the comparable figures for independence were 27.7; 56.3; and 16 per cent respectively. They were determined, however, to be more precise in terms of party support:

'Let us now get down to the main issue. Did the Péquiste voters turn to that party in support of its constitutional choice? Is the same true of the Liberal voters?

'Taking into account that attitudes to federalism and independence are not on the same basis for the voters, the best approach is to tackle the question in relation to each of the two options. There is another reason for this approach, our wish to make the logical distinctions between necessary and sufficient conditions.'

They summarized the result of their poll in the following tables. Still not content after the election, the pollsters asked whether a vote cast for the Liberals or the Péquistes was because of their constitutional position or satisfaction with the Bourassa government. Eighty-one per cent of the Liberal voters replied 'the constitution' and 40 per cent 'satisfaction with the government'; 68 per cent of those who voted PQ mentioned the constitution and 53 per cent their dissatisfaction with the government.

The aftermath

Only a Molière could have done justice to the comedy played by the Créditistes after the election. By the end of the year Samson, the previous leader, was expelled by the Dupuis faction, a convention had dumped Dupuis, and Caouette had called a convention of the Quebec wing of the federal party for early 1974 to see what could be done. The Union nationale continued to mumble about the need for a real 'regroupement,' and M. Dupuis agreed to have it considered by a Créditiste convention. Quebec Tories looked at the shambles of the non-separatist opposition to the Liberals and flew a number of kites to test the wind for a provincial Conservative party that might provide a federal base. Louis Laberge stated on October 31 that the trade unions had to take on the role of opposition, and Marcel Pepin urged the creation of a network of citizens committees throughout Quebec 'to give workers the voice they won't have in the National Assembly.'

***La Presse* polls of PQ and Liberal supporters**

Tendency to vote for the PQ as a percentage of support for independence and support for federalism

	PQ	Other parties	Total
Montreal			
Independentists	83	17	100
Not independentists	15	85	100
Federalists	13	87	100
Not federalists	66	34	100
Rest of Quebec			
Independentists	63	37	100
Not independentists	9	91	100
Federalists	12	88	100
Not federalists	46	54	100

Tendency to vote for the Liberals as a percentage of support for independence and support for federalism

	LIBERALS	Other parties	Total
Montreal			
Independentists	13	87	100
Not independentists	71	29	100
Federalists	74	26	100
Not federalists	28	72	100
Rest of Quebec			
Independentists	20	80	100
Not independentists	70	30	100
Federalists	68	32	100
Not federalists	34	66	100

While some members of the Parti québécois spoke of the need to form a parallel opposition outside the Assembly, Lévesque took his defeat gracefully. 'Thousands of Quebeckers understood what the PQ offers ... and one day we will penetrate the last fears and complexes which prevent so many from seeing how beautiful and fruitful life as a nation would be.' Other members, however, were more concerned about the present: should Lévesque run in a seat vacated by one of the victorious Péquistes? should the party modify its separatist stance? should it modify its social and economic platform? should a separatist daily be established in Montreal to combat *Le Devoir*, whose editor had betrayed the nation by finally opting for federalism? These and other questions were considered at a meeting on November 3-4 in Montreal and at a National Council meeting on November 17-18 in Quebec.

By the end of the year a number of questions had been answered. René Lévesque was not going to run for the Assembly. A new Montreal daily was to be established with defeated candidate Yves Michaud at its head. Jacques-Yvan Morin was selected as the House leader after Lévesque had intervened to break a deadlock between Morin and the more radical Burns. As André Larocque bitterly remarked, the group in the Assembly would remain 'the big speech-making boys.' And despite André Normandeau's blunt reflection that a radically revised federal system and linguistic policy might be more suited to the political realities in Quebec (*Le Devoir*, October 31) and Claude Morin's rhetorical question whether independence in stages might not be better accepted (*Le Devoir*, November 17) no basic changes had been announced by the end of the year. There was no doubt, however, that the issues would arise in 1974. M. Normandeau, defeated in Mont-Royal on October 29, stated that 'the choice of a democratic-socialist Quebec which will be culturally more independent than ever within an economic Canadian federation deserves attention from members and PQ sympathizers over the next four years. I am personally committed to defend these ideas in the PQ and take them as far as a leadershiip convention if necessary.' Nor were Claude Morin or Jacques Parizeau, who resigned from the executive committee on November 23, likely to remain silent on major matters of policy.

On election night Premier Bourassa pledged his government to secure the cultural independence of a Quebec that remained economically linked to Canada. The message was repeated in a full-page letter published in Quebec newspapers on November 3:

'Fundamentally this election of October 29, 1973 carries a three-fold message.

'It shows the clear and unequivocal approval by Quebeckers of the main policies of the Quebec Liberal Party; the permanence of our belief in the Canadian Federal system and the pursuit of our primary objective of economic development which represents the foundations of the balanced progress of our society and of the efficiency of our social and cultural policies.

'The election also underlines, we believe, the desire of Quebeckers to see their government preoccupy itself even more with the true improvement of the quality of life of every citizen, specially the underpriviledged (*sic*) of our society. Everyone agrees that governments cannot do everythiing for the citizen and certainly should not try to do everything that citizens themselves must do; the government must, however, allow citizens from all regions of Quebec to face the realities of our time and assure them security, prosperity, and liberty.

'The election also shows us the importance of the future of the French language and culture; they allow the maintenance of an essential and legitimate pride which, in turn, assures the progress of the Quebec community and the stability of Canada.

'We will have to answer, with justice and realism, this undeniable need of French-speaking Quebeckers for cultural security and sovereignty. The Liberal party of Quebec, which received the support of all groups in our society, is specially well-placed to perform this duty.

'Quebec has an imperious necessity in this regard; we want to fully answer it. All Canada is itself profoundly concerned with this question and we are confident that all Canadians will co-operate fully in the search of solutions.

'Our policies, in this vital area for the future of Quebec and Canada, will never be directed against anyone. On the contrary, we will strive to associate all concerned in the search for practical, effective, and just solutions which will reinforce the solidarity of all Quebeckers and in turn the unity of our country, Canada.'

Some indication of what Premier Bourassa and his government meant by cultural sovereignty could be seen in the position adopted on communications at the November 29-30 federal-provincial conference.

In the Liberal platform during the election and after his victory Premier Bourassa indicated his willingness – even his desire – to reopen discussions on the constitution. And when he and Prime Minister Trudeau announced they would meet at 24 Sussex on November 2 the assumption was that the discussion would turn to the constitution. Asked in the Commons on October 31 whether there would be such discussions the prime minister replied that if 'the new government of Quebec can present propositions compatible with the federal position and generally acceptable to Canadians, we will be extremely happy to resume constitutional conferences.' Earlier in the year the prime minister, in his first interview with *Le Devoir* since his election in 1968, outlined his position on a return to Victoria:

'Q: Mr Trudeau, my allotted time is nearly up, but there are still two questions I would like to ask. The first has to do with constitutional reform, in limbo since the failure of the Victoria Conference. At the time, you let it be known that you would be extremely hesitant to open this Pandora's box – 'this can of worms' was your expression. Has your stand on this issue changed at all?

'A: No, I would still be very hesitant. And my reservations at the time were in line with warnings I had issued in '67 and '68. When it was the vogue for provincial governments to call for constitutional review I reminded them and anyone who wanted to listen that the review initiated at the beginning of the 1960s and culminating in the Fulton-Favreau formula had, if my memory serves, been agreed to and later rejected by the Lesage government. In the months before Victoria we thought we were very close to an understanding, not only with all the western provinces but with Quebec as well, and it was Quebec that caused the failure of the Victoria Conference. So twice in two years ... personally, I would have a lot of reservations about opening a new series of constitutional conferences. I was going to add ... unless the Quebec government makes some overtures and indicates routes to possible agreement.

'Q: Perhaps I might suggest one possible route: a thorough consideration of the question that concerns Quebec most, that of the division of powers – even if the notion of special status to which you yourself are opposed were set aside – in the light of effectiveness. In the present context of inflation, for example, we note that the federal government lacks the full powers it would need for controlling prices, supposing it decided price controls were useful. Again, regarding competition, recourse has to be to the Criminal Code, which may not be the most effective approach. And so on. Looking at all these examples, one realizes that not all the power transfers we might envisage are from Ottawa to the provinces; they could often be from the provinces to Ottawa as well.

'A: Yes, but the very areas you have just listed are ones where we have in fact launched studies and often completed them. In the conferences before Victoria we advanced proposals in areas such as those you mention, proposals which would have meant transfers in both directions. You will recall that the beginning of the final stage, possibly seven or eight months before Victoria, came when everyone said: fine, instead of three, five, or six years of meetings to study all these areas (the ones you list and many more), let's try to settle on the amending formula, entrench basic rights including language rights, and repatriate the constitution – afterwards, with our amending instrument, we will be able to resume discussion. When we found an amending formula that was acceptable to Quebec, I thought the business was settled. With a veto on all amendments, Quebec was in a very good position to negotiate not only with the other provinces but with Canada as well, and tell them: "If you want amendments favouring the central government, then let's have some favouring the provincial governments too." Ah well, I refer you back to your contacts in the Quebec government ...

'Q: So for the moment it's up to Quebec to take the initiative in reopening the constitutional question?

'A: Yes.'

By the end of the year M. Bourassa and his Liberal government remained even more enigmatic than before. To some, constitutional reform and cultural sovereignty were simply euphemisms for the continued movement towards a status for Quebec that was only a hairline removed from René Lévesque's Souveraineté association. Whether one looked at the Liberal platform or the Parti québécois' popular vote Claude Ryan's warning to the Bank of Nova Scotia shareholders that 'the result must be interpreted as a mandate for action, not as an invitation to complacency' seemed appropriate (Halifax *Chronicle-Herald*, December 15). And given the reaction of English Canadians like Mr Braithwaite, who was by no means alone on the morrow of the election, Pierre Chauveau's lamentful observation comes to mind: 'English and French, we climb by a double flight of stairs towards the destinies reserved for us on this continent, without knowing each other, without meeting each other, and without even seeing each other, except on the landing of politics.' Chauveau was the first post-Confederation premier of the province of Quebec.

1974

Separation by stages

The federal election of July 8 returned the Liberals with a majority as the Prime Minister sagely lectured the voter on the futility of wage and price controls. While Quebec benefited from M. Bourassa's 'profitable federalism' with a cushioned price for oil and a $3 billion regional development agreement, the steady war of attrition against Ottawa continued unabated. M. L'Allier's shock troops continued the attack on communications, and Jean Bienvenue deployed his forces to secure a provincial voice over immigration. But the major weapon in the battle for cultural sovereignty came with Bill 22 in Quebec. After almost a decade of controversy, experimentation, legislation, pleading, and threats, the francisation programme was not working – at least not fast enough – and not only immigrant children but also francophones were continuing to be educated in English. Bill 22 made French the official language of the province; required that French be the language of normal usage in government; and legislated the use of French in all the externals of the business world and bribed and bullied its use in internal operations. But it was the educational provisions that excited fierce controversy. Bill 22 required that French be the language of instruction in the public schools, and that the teaching of English could neither begin nor cease without the approval of the minister. While children of anglophone parents could continue to be educated in English, children without English as their mother tongue would go to French schools. Nationalists denounced the limited freedom of choice; anglophone and immigrant deplored the restrictions and the objectives.

The overwhelming victory of the Liberals in 1973 did nothing to dampen the spirits of the Péquistes, accompanied as it had been by a sharp increase in the popular vote for the PQ. However, René Lévesque's personal defeat, the realization that many supporters were not separatists, the suspicion that without a broader base the party was doomed to be a perpetual minority, the conflict over where the wider base should be found, and the differences that had emerged during and after the campaign about the approach to independence itself, all caused considerable anxiety and tension within the party in 1974.

On February 28 the first issue of *Le Jour* appeared as scheduled. The daily was financed by 875 separate shareholders owning 2150 shares and a public appeal that netted $250,000 in less than three months. René Lévesque and Jacques Parizeau were among the directors. Yves Michaud was editor, and the staff consisted largely of separatist journalists hired from other Montreal dailies. Despite the heavy competition in Montreal it was clear almost from the beginning that *Le Jour* would stay alive. A similar sign of party vitality came with the sixth annual fundraising drive. The month-long drive, L'Opération Ressource, raised $824,000 from almost forty thousand individual donors. Perhaps more significant was René Lévesque's appearance in February at a major labour rally for the striking United Aircraft workers. Dominique Clift wrote (*Montreal Star,* February 16):

'The decision to avoid being identified with organized labour had been both a tactical and ideological one. It coincided with a period in the party's life when Lévesque was liquidating the radical elements who believed in the political effectiveness of street demonstrations and who professed a certain sympathy with the use of violence as a political weapon ... Lévesque has always believed that violence in any form was regressive and counterproductive. His political aims were to court the so-called silent majority, and demonstrate the realism of his economic and social program for independence. He sought to be both respectable and reassuring.' Lévesque's appearance at the rally seemed to suggest that after the 1973 election the radical wing led by Robert Burns had at last persuaded Lévesque that the PQ had to shed its tie-and-jacket approach and secure more support among the workers and trade unionists. The party also attempted to build up its base by taking the lead in organizing a coalition of forces to defeat Mayor Drapeau.

One major question was resolved on May 18 when René Lévesque announced that he would remain at the head of the PQ if the November national congress confirmed him in that position. For the moment, at least, the attempt to keep the PQ both socialist and nationalist, to keep it respectable without necessarily preventing links with various discontented groups to help forge an anti-Bourassa alliance and keep the party more or less united, would continue. But whatever relief the party may have felt that its inner tensions would continue to be tempered by Lévesque's moderation, diplomacy, and general prestige soon ended. Early in September, on the eve of the annual meeting of the party's 350-member National council, Robert Burns, the radical and outspoken member of the National Assembly, stated in an interview that Lévesque was politically handicapped by his two defeats and suggested that unless he could win a seat before the next election he should step down. At the same time the press carried reports that four of the MNAs were dissatisfied with Lévesque's leadership. Among those reportedly critical of Lévesque was Marcel Léger, the MNA for Lafontaine, PQ whip in the Assembly, and member of the national executive, who published an article in *Le Jour* on September 6 condemning the party leadership for failing to pay attention to party organization. M. Léger was convinced that only three years of hard work on organization and politicisation in the constituencies would lead to a victory in 1977:

'Unhappily, the reaction of most executive members (not all of them, fortunately) came as added confirmation to me that the executive's concerns could not be farther from organizational concerns, and are still focused only on intellectual and technical matters, a million miles away from practical, methodical achievements. A year after the '73 election we are where we were a year following the '70 election; this is why I am once more raising before the national council and/or national convention the question of the emphasis that must be given to organization in a party that aims to take office.

'It is both an advantage and a handicap for the Parti québécois that its leadership includes university people, thinkers, intellectuals, and senior civil servants from former governments, who have given the idea of independence the required credibility and weight that allowed us to develop from the marginal third party we were in the beginning, to become a party that is now the official Opposition, not merely in Quebec, but to the federal regime in Ottawa.'

The PQ national executive met on September 7-8 at Mont Joli. Regretting that Robert Burns had not attended and that Léger and Les-

sard had spoken out critically of the party executive, M. Lévesque asserted that he would remain at the head of the party and would be a
candidate for the presidency at the November convention. However,
without altering his view of the dangers of a permanent party organization he did agree to a proposal to establish a ten-member provincial
strategy committee to plan the creation of riding organizations. The
party also undertook a drive to increase party membership from seventy thousand to one hundred thousand.

But at a press conference on September 13 Lévesque struck back
at his critics. He tabled his lengthy report to the council at Mont Joli
and warned that unless the party stopped its internal squabbling it
would start to fall apart, and he personally had no desire to preside
over a decline. However, he added that he intended to fight for the
presidency, and in the best western tradition dared his enemies to
come and get him. While suggesting that no member of the assembly
seemed ready to challenge for the leadership, he did admit that some
of the criticism of him was justified. He agreed that the party organization could be improved, but warned of the dangers of a machine and
observed that organization, though it might be a necessity, 'is not a
panacea and above all not an absolute. On its own, neither a miracle
of organization nor any other miracle will ever bring the PQ to power.'
One of the major problems was the difficulty of dividing jurisdiction
and responsibility between the national executive and council and the
parliamentary wing, he said, reiterating that the national council ran
the party on behalf of the membership and that between councils the
national executive was the ruling body. He warned of the dangers of
too close an association but did suggest a division of authority, the
parliamentary group dwelling largely on parliamentary work and the
national executive being much more active in extralegislative tasks
and constituency organization. On September 28-9 the national executive met the six-man parliamentary group in a Sorel hotel. The parties
clearly had not agreed, but emerged from the twenty-four hours of
talk with a 'better understanding', and planned to meet every two
months to talk things over.

There was more public unanimity, however, over a 'revision' of the
Parti québécois programme for the achievement of independence.
During the 1973 election campaign the party had indicated that a referendum would follow a PQ victory, but the party itself had never
officially altered its position or at least clarified its position to end any
ambiguity. After the election many members of the party began to ad-

vocate a staged approach to independence as a way of securing the support of people frightened by independence itself. According to Alain Duhamel of *Le Jour* (April 8), the national council meeting on April 7-8 decided that the national congress in November would 'redefine the process of attaining independence and be more accessible to the general public.

'Without compromising the PQ's basic choice, the delegates to the National Council have wanted to devote some effort to defining the process of attaining independence. The whole referendum question, about which there has been some confusion since the last election campaign, will be thoroughly examined. The question will be debated previously in a series of regional conventions to be held through May and June. It will be the beginning of a comprehensive reconsideration of all the steps leading to independence after the Parti québécois gains power.

'The delegates to these conventions will have to decide the extent to which gaining power in itself constitutes a referendum on independence, or on equal opportunities for Québécois, or both; and by how many stages, over what period of time, the Québécois "yes" vote for self-determination is to be brought into effect.'

One of the leading advocates of separation in stages was Claude Morin, who had been asked to prepare a working document by the national executive. His own position was revealed in a lengthy paper published in *La Presse* on September 26. M. Morin argued that the party had to clarify the ambiguities in its programme: 'without in any way bringing our basic choice into question, it is essential for the party to demonstrate its intention of guiding Quebec to a state of sovereignty in a manner that is closer to the Québécois environment and Québécois thinking, and thus more acceptable to our population.'

Morin underlined that the actual transfer of power and people from Ottawa would take time:

'The proclamation by the National Assembly of the principle of Quebec's sovereignty immediately following the party's victory, as now provided for in our platform, will not exempt us from the imperatives imposed by time. It will mark the formal beginning of the process of accession to sovereignty, but this simple move will not in itself equip Quebec with all the attributes, material and judicial, required for the practical, day-by-day exercise of sovereignty. Similarly, we would be wrong in thinking that the mere election of the party would mean Quebec's on-the-spot, automatic acquisition of powers and resources, now federal, which are essential if that sovereignty is to be real.'

Then the man who had encountered federal officials at countless bargaining tables laid down his strategy and scenario for the realization of independence:

'The achievement of sovereignty, then, cannot be instantaneous or swift, still less abrupt. This is one more reason for making a start on it very shortly after taking office.

'No matter what plan is set up for the achievement of sovereignty, in explaining it we must avoid giving people the disturbing impression that future developments are to be locked into a rigid and theoretical programme, formed as if tomorrow could bring us nothing that has not already been taken into account. It is also important to make our pledge that the people will not be pushed ...

'As soon as it have been elected and held this vote of principle, a Péquiste government must call on Ottawa to transfer powers to Quebec under jointly established procedures. However, it is neither possible nor necessary here to "programme" the whole transfer operation in detail. This would tie us to an artificial schedule.

'Can Ottawa stubbornly refuse the required transfers? Here, let us not make the mistake of minimizing the political impact on Canada of the election of a government with the mandate of achieving Quebec sovereignty. There will be no question, in discussions with Ottawa, of an avowedly federalist provincial administration subject to century-old rules, but rather an independentist government (provisionally provincial) chosen democratically by the population.

'Since it will have the power, and especially since it will be determined to move forward, a Péquiste government will be in a position to make moves that Ottawa will find hard to counter. It will be able to apply pressure. Anyone who is unable to imagine anything more extreme than a province given to verbal confrontation (this has occurred frequently and with limited effect) cannot then be aware of the decisive impact that can be made by constant and varied activity from a province truly wanting control of political power, as Quebec would be, on the operation of the current Canadian system.

'I have said that our sovereignty can in practice derive only from a transfer of powers from Ottawa to Quebec. I have just mentioned the possible pressure a Péquiste government could bring to bear on Ottawa, in such a way, let us say, as to stimulate action. Yet in the last analysis, what is Quebec's strength as against Ottawa's? What can dislodge the federal government?

'Do we plan an armed struggle to get by force what we are refused by other means? No.

'Then what can we look to for getting things moving? The political determination of our government and popular support. The political determination will make our elected representatives show firmness and apply pressure to Ottawa. It is popular support, however, that will supply our public men with their strength. Our leverage will come from public opinion and nothing else.

'The real question, then, is how a Péquiste government can be assured of continuous, decisive support from Québécois public opinion.

'First of all, obviously, it will have to provide satisfactory administration of the Quebec state. Beyond this perfectly natural prerequisite, however, there is the necessity of working out a close relation with the people from the very moment of gaining power. Experience tells us that an informed Québécois population naturally sides with the government of Quebec. (Examples: "provincial autonomy" with M. Duplessis, fiscal sharing and the pension scheme with M. Lesage, constitutional review with Messrs Johnson and Bertrand, the rejection of Victoria with M. Bourassa.) This is why, in any exchange with Ottawa, a Péquiste administration must let the citizens know what is going on, and do so to an extent never before known.

'The support expressed by the election is quite adequate for setting in motion the process of accession to sovereignty. Actually, the practical difficulty will not be starting Quebec's movement towards sovereignty, but doing so in such a way that it will keep on going.

'Though we won't have to step automatically into every trap laid for us, we can expect, in strictly practical terms, that a Péquiste government will, in the course of moving towards sovereignty, feel the need to seek explicit confirmation of popular support.

'In fact, our advance rejection of such reinforcement means depriving Péquiste government of the popular support that is its most constant requirement. This would not be altogether bright. Moreover, this refusal might be seen as a confession of weakness, and an indication that the government fears the opinion of the people.

'Finally, if our platform does not include the explicit possibility of such a "vote of confidence" during the process of gaining sovereignty, the present electorate could form the impression that the election of a Péquiste government would be irrevocable, absolutely decisive, in a sense a final act.

'Can sovereignty be made complete during the party's first term in

office? If there are no delays, and no serious internal problems mo-
nopolize government energies, it is possible. At all events we must begin our exercise of power in the full determination that it will be so.
Just as possibly, however, at least as regards a number of delicate
and complex questions, this transformation of Quebec may be completed in a second term. Let us not forget that the people will expect
independence to be realized in an orderly way, without any shocks, by
a gradual transfer of powers.

'In other words, with the independence process under way but not
yet complete, the Parti québécois might very well have to call another
election which, whether we want it or not, would give the voters another chance to pronounce on sovereignty.

'Given the unavoidable material constraints weighing on the move
towards sovereignty, plus the dynamism which the party's arrival in
office will give the Quebec-Ottawa politics and the normal party-politi-
cal interplay in Quebec itself, we face the following situation: for whatever reason (confirmation of popular support, the need to accelerate
the transfer of powers or, quite simply, a normal Quebec election at or
before the end of the first term of office), a Péquiste government will
find it useful or appropriate or necessary, depending on the circumstances, to consult the people while accession to sovereignty is still in
process.

'Some are worrying whether open recognition of the democratic
need for a fresh consultation of the people would give all our federalist opponents a "last chance" to sabotage our plan. In this regard I
can offer two comments, or perhaps two questions, based on the plain
fact that the election of a Péquiste government would certainly not
mean suspension of the normal functioning of parties and institutions,
or the activities of our opponents, or, of course, our supporters. On
one hand, can we seriously think that our federalist opponents will
consider themselves conclusively beaten by a single election result,
particularly as this result may well not be as conclusive as we would
wish? And on the other hand, facing these same opponents, how
would a Péquiste government look if it seemed reluctant to go back to
its supreme source of support, Québécois opinion?

'Chances are, then, that a Péquiste government will have to consult
the people along the way, before sovereignty is complete. This being
the case, why not say so clearly in our platform, even make it a promise? This would both attest to our democratic concern and, – which is
by no means negligible – reassure those of our fellow citizens inclined
to "try" us just so long as they were allowed to "wait and see."

'This proposal in no way undermines our plan or delays its fulfilment (quite the reverse, it is liable to speed it up), and can easily be explained.

'Given all this, we should make some modifications in our present platform. So that it can easily be seen how they work in context, I reproduce the clauses in question, italicizing changes and additions. A Parti québécois government is committed to:

1/ Set in motion immediately the process of accession to sovereignty when this has been proclaimed by the National Assembly – the transfer of powers and transfer of jurisdictions *to begin without delay* – opposing any federal interference as contrary to the right of self-determination of peoples.

2/ *Democratically continue and complete Quebec's accession to sovereignty while assuring itself along the way of the explicit support of the Québécois by an unequivocal referendum or, if need be, a new election.*

3/ Ask *the population* to approve a constitution worked out with participation by citizens at the riding level *and ratified* by delegates to a constituent assembly.

'I have cut the reference to a referendum Ottawa might set up at the level of Canada since the context seems explicit enough to me. Regarding the referendum on the Quebec constitution, I have cut the words 'to make this independence concrete' as being no longer necessary. Also in clause 3, I have cut the word 'referendum' to avoid any confusion with the same word in the preceding clause. Still in clause 3, I have added the words 'and ratified' to make the sense clearer. The other clauses in this section remain unaltered, but will need renumbering.

'The wording suggested here does not have to be final. Its primary purpose at this point is to show what the issues are.'

The programme for achieving independence was debated at length at the Sorel weekend meeting between the executive and the parliamentary wing and the following text approved: 'A Parti Québécois government is committed to:

1/ Bring before the National Assembly shortly after its election a bill authorizing it to: (*a*) demand from Ottawa repatriation to Quebec of all powers, except those the two governments shall, in view of economic association, decide to entrust to mutual bodies; (*b*) in view of this objective, enter into technical discussions with Ottawa on the orderly transfer of jurisdictions; (*c*) work out agreements with Canada regarding in particular the division of assets and liabilities and the ownership of public property, in conformity with the accepted norms of international law.

2/ In the event of wholesale opposition from Ottawa, systematically assume the exercise of all the powers of a sovereign state, first assuring itself of the support of the Québécois by means of a referendum.

3/ Submit to the population a national constitution prepared by delegates to a constituent assembly.

'Clauses 4, 5, and 6 of the present platform remain unchanged.'

The debate over the referendum continued with increasing bitterness until the November convention. On the eve of the convention *La Presse* (November 14) published the results of a major poll conducted in mid-October by L'Institut québécois d'opinion publique. On the question of independence the results were shown in the accompanying table. The French split 52.5 to 31 per cent against independence, with 16.5 per cent failing to answer, while the English voted 87 to 7 with 6 per cent not answering. The total vote for independence was highest in Quebec where 36 per cent favoured independence, while the vote in Montreal and the rest of the province was only 27.5 and 26 per cent respectively. Independence was by far the most popular among the eighteen to twenty-four age group, of whom 58 per cent were in favour, while less than 25 per cent of the twenty-five to forty-

Quebec attitudes to independence October 1974, percentages

	Total	Lib.	PQ	Cred.	UN
For	28	10.5	61	21.6	13
Against	57.5	76.5	26	63	82.5
Don't know or no response	14.5	13	13	15.5	4.5

SOURCE: *La Presse* poll

Quebec preference for a referendum on independence October 1974, percentages

	Total	Lib.	PQ	Cred.	UN
Yes	83	83	83	84.5	84.5
No	11	12	14.5	11	11
No resp.	6	5	2.5	4.5	4.5

SOURCE: *La Presse* poll

four, and well under 20 per cent of those forty-five and over, supported independence. At the same time, however, the voting intention question revealed that while 28 per cent would vote PQ, only 29 per cent would vote Liberal, 5 per cent for both the UN and the Créditistes, while 27.5 per cent refused to reply or did not know. French-speaking Canadians split 30.5 to 27.5 per cent for the PQ.

The poll also indicated that the executive was correct in assuming the people wanted a referendum: 'If the Parti québécois took office following the next provincial election, would you say that they ought to consult the population before moving for independence, or would you say that this would not be necessary?' (See the second table.) The figures corresponded closely to those released by Lévesque on October 17 and taken before the October 1973 election when 87.3 per cent of the Péquistes and 74.6 per cent of Liberals said they were more or less in favour of the principle of a referendum (*La Presse*, October 18). Surprisingly, the anglophones felt it was less necessary to consult the people than did the francophones, by a margin of 3 per cent.

Opening the conference in the glow of the *La Presse* poll and the breakthrough in the Montreal civic elections partially engineered by the PQ, Lévesque appealed for party unity. The convention was reasonably docile, following Lévesque's advice not to rewrite the party programme and engage in ideological debates. Not only was an enlarged executive elected composed largely of his supporters but the congress voted 630 to 353 in favour of the document on the referendum. When it was over Lévesque described it as 'the finest, most productive, most balanced, and calmest in the party's history,' and congratulated the delegates for reconciling 'the gut aspect of their convictions with the necessary calculations of strategy.'

Thus 1974 ended for the PQ with Marcel Léger off and running to create a new organization, independence remaining the ultimate end of PQ policy, but the party able to soft-pedal independence and attract the growing anti-Bourassa elements. Yet there were many party militants somewhat militantly watching Lévesque and the leadership to make sure they were not going soft on independence.

1975

Power or principle

Early in the year Premier Bourassa informed readers of *Le Monde diplomatique* that 'Quebec had set itself the ambition of being and remaining a French state within the Canadian common market.' He promised Canadians that he would 'fight separatism to the end of my career,' but asked English Canadians to understand that he could not 'allow our cultural survival to depend on the good will of the majority ... I cannot do things differently. My margin for manoeuvre is very small. I am working to consolidate a besieged society.' The strains began to show. In Ottawa, L'Allier was able to create a common provincial position on the communications front, but in view of the refusal of the federal government to concede defeat he downgraded his status at the conference to that of an observer. In Quebec the controversy over Bill 22 continued and Jerome Choquette resigned from the cabinet when it would not completely abolish freedom of choice for immigrants. For most Quebeckers, however, inflation and unemployment, the enormous debt for the Olympics and James Bay, and massive labour unrest were of more immediate concern than the nationalist's battle of words.

Despite its deliberately low profile, the Parti québécois never seemed stronger. The faltering Liberal leadership, which led even the friendly Roger Lemelin to address a front-page editorial in *La Presse* to the premier – 'We're waiting for a prime minister. Monsieur Bourassa is at the crossroads' – the shadows and realities of scandal, and the divisions within the party made the Péquistes look better regardless of

La Presse, September 4, 1975

their separatism and encouraged increased discussion of a new political party. A poll carried out by the Centre de Recherche de l'Opinion
Publique for the cbc between April 28 and May 2 revealed that of
1,011 francophones 24.8 per cent stated they would vote Péquiste
and 21.2 per cent Liberal, although 45.1 per cent did not know or refused to respond. At the same time, however, a poll carried out for the
Liberal party by the Institut Québécois de l'Opinion Publique stated
that voting intentions among 984 francophones (83 per cent) and anglophones favoured the Liberals 30.5 to 23 per cent. Among the francophones alone the Liberals led the pq 29 to 25.5 per cent (*Le Devoir*,
May 26). On the other hand a Gallup Poll released on February 12 indicated that only 40 per cent of Quebeckers believed that separatism
was growing, a figure that had declined from 51 per cent in 1970.

Throughout the year the Péquistes concentrated, not on nationalist
rhetoric, but on constant attacks on the alleged corruption and real
lack of leadership of the Bourassa government. A large-scale radio
and tv campaign and support for *Le Jour* were made possible by a
spring fund-raising campaign which grossed $912,000. Moral support
for *Le Jour* came from the press across Canada when Donald Macdo-
nald cancelled energy conservation advertising because, as he said,
''it seems to me that a newspaper which proposes the destruction of
Canada should not expect the support of the federal government for
its efforts.' The Montreal *Gazette* (March 27) reminded Ottawa that

'the expression of opinion urging the independence of a province from the rest of Canada is no crime. The principle of freedom of expression is indivisible; it cannot be upheld in general and attacked in particular.' Christopher Young wrote in the *Ottawa Citizen* (March 29) that 'if separatism cannot be argued peacefully on the editorial page of a newspaper, then it will be argued violently in the streets. If *Le Jour* is driven out of business, or even appears to be driven out of business, by the ruthless exercise of federal power, that will only help to revive old passions and renew old wounds that had seemed to be slowly healing.'

The weakening grasp of the Bourassa government increased rather than lessened the divisions over strategy within the Parti québécois. In 1974, after bitter in-fighting, the party had agreed to hold a referendum on independence after its victory at the polls. But to some members of the party, such as Pierre Bourgault (who re-emerged during the year), the primacy of power over principle was abhorrent. Moreover, the November 1974 resolution remained unclear. To some it still equated victory and independence, while others agreed with Claude Morin, one of the leading spokesmen for the 'campaign-time wing' or the 'beat Bourassa first' wing, that 'as far as the PQ is concerned it is certain and understood, normal and decided that there will be no question of going for independence if the citizens don't want it. This is a democratic assurance given to the people in black and white; it is an explicit commitment' (*Le Devoir*, September 23).

Morin's statement seemed to further confuse the issue and change
the question from one of procedure to one of policy, and there was an
immediate outburst within the party. The Montreal Centre executive
accused Morin of a 'mistaken, unwarranted interpretation' and declared that 'separation of the assumption of power from the necessity
of achieving independence means abandoning the overall plan for
changing Quebec society that is in the party platform.' Finally, in an
attempt to quell the dispute, the national executive and the parliamentary wing issued the following statement on October 8:

'The Parti québécois was founded to free Quebec from the state of
economic and political dependence endangering its cultural identity
and blocking its development. Our aim is to make Quebec a sovereign
state holding all the powers and resources it needs to solve its devel-
opmental problems and bring into being the kind of society appropriate to it. The aim of independence is the prime reason for the Parti
québécois' existence and there can be no question of our losing sight
of this in any way.

'Yet reasonable people will recognize that the obvious prerequisite
for our attaining this objective is gaining power.

'This is imperative as well, just as obviously, because of a political
conjuncture in which Quebec is being drawn more than ever before
into a state of servility and powerlessness that could become irrevocable. Hackneyed and corrupt, the Bourassa administration reveals its
total incapacity to offer Québécois objectives with the faintest chance
of rallying them, restoring to them that impetus and self-confidence
without which no genuine development can get under way. Everywhere there is a growing sense of this urgent need to get moving
again.

'It is important, then, to make an immediate start on this first part of
our task, the overthrow of an old party that is degrading and demoral-
izing us.

'At the same time we will have taken the essential giant step to open
the way to the actual achievement of independence. But this will not
mean that the independence has been achieved. Our platform makes
it clear that the election of the Parti québécois will not at the same moment, at a single blow, produce instant sovereignty. Whatever happens, there will inevitably be a transition period during which it will be
absolutely necessary to make sure as well that a majority of Québécois are in agreement with their government. Yet have they not always
been so when it was a question of repossessing powers? Is there a

single true Québécois who does not want us to become masters in our own house as soon as possible?

'According to even the most optimistic hypotheses, this obligatory transition period will last for some time. Before the planned negotiations can be begun, we will have to secure the agreement of the National Assembly and then open discussions with Ottawa. We will have to assemble our briefs for these negotiations and allow them a reasonable time to bear fruit.

'But by far the most probable eventuality is that Ottawa will refuse to enter into or follow through on such negotiations. Thus, the Parti québécois' platform includes a clearly stated and firm commitment not to proceed with independence without having first assured itself by referendum of the support of the Québécois, so that everyone, here as elsewhere, knows that we are together for this new episode in our history.

'Clearly, then, whatever the hypothesis, the Parti québécois will use power to achieve independence democratically, and just as clearly, it will attempt, during the transition period, to make maximum use of all the present provincial powers to invigorate our political atmosphere and solve all problems that can be solved in this context.'

The militants refused to accept the position, however, and in *Le Jour* (October 16) André LeCorre wrote a scathing denunciation of the moderates. The PQ had been betrayed by leaders who had deserted basic principles for an electoral gain of what he estimated would at best be twenty-five seats and 37 per cent of the vote. If independence was not mandatory, he warned, non-separatists would run as candidates and everyone would be dead before Claude Morin finished negotiations with Ottawa. M. LeCorre continued the battle at the meeting of the National Council at Victoriaville on October 18-19, where he and others were savagely attacked by René Lévesque for fussing over worn-out issues ('chewing old rags'). The position taken in the October 8 statement was approved by the Council with only four dissenting votes, but a second resolution moved by M. LeCorre which would have reopened the question was only defeated 51 to 32.

1976

Home run: The election of November 15

'Give me one good reason why there should be an election,' said Benoit Payeur, the newly elected president of the Quebec Liberal party, on August 30. It was difficult to find a reason, and even the obvious one – that the Liberals thought they could win – was not only inappropriate but dubious. Yet six weeks later Robert Bourassa announced that he was seeking a new mandate to face the challenge of Trudeau in Ottawa and the trade unions in Quebec. No one expected the Liberals to emerge unscathed. No one anticipated the slaughter of November 15.

Background to decision

Tanned and buoyant, Premier Bourassa returned from a Miami vacation on January 12 and announced that there would be no election in 1976. The decision made eminent sense for the Bourassa government was riding on a wave of unprecedented unpopularity. A reliable poll taken in October 1975 indicated that 28.8 per cent intended to vote for the Parti québécois and 24 per cent for the Liberals. Although 32.7 per cent refused to reply or did not know, only the most optimistic Liberal could take any comfort in the results. Moreover, the government faced economic, social, and cultural problems of enormous proportions and complexity.

Since the 1973 election nothing had seemed to go right for the Liberals. Inflation had escalated the cost of James Bay – Bourassa's 'project of the century' – from $5.8 billion in 1971 to over $16 billion by

1976 with no end in sight. Maladministration, if not corruption, helped inflation push the cost of the Olympics from $250 million to something approaching $1.5 billion. While the Bourassa government was hardly to blame, it was forced to pick up the pieces. Nor was high unemployment largely the government's fault, but it did nothing to lessen social tension or increase revenue. Labour relations continued to be the worst in the country and by 1975-76 Quebec accounted for 41 per cent of all work stoppages in Canada. The government not only faced the implacable hostility of the three large trade union organizations, but the contracts of the militant construction workers and public service employees had to be renegotiated in 1976.

The government's commission on organized crime had helped to identify and diagnose the disease, but it had also revealed that some Liberal politicians had not always been discreet at election time. Other inquiries, planned or not, suggested that contract tendering was not always beyond reproach, that lottery distributors made fortunes doing nothing, that prominent Liberals belonged to companies with lucrative dealings with the Quebec liquor commission, and, like most governments, that the Liberals kept a list of preferred lawyers and accountants on whom it bestowed its favours. Finally, the educational provisions of Bill 22 continued to satisfy neither French, English, nor immigrant, and played havoc with the internal unity of the party and the cabinet.

The March 16 throne speech did not suggest that the government had found the answers to the major problems facing the province, or that it planned to go to the people. Premier Bourassa promised to oppose unilateral federal action on the patriation of the British North America Act and to demand a new equalization formula; to create departments of tourism and recreation and population and immigration; to prepare green papers on cultural policy, education, and urban transportation, to introduce new consumer protection laws, and to pump more money into Crown corporations to increase their participation in the economy. Among the top priorities, however, were the anti-inflation programme and the contract negotiations with the three hundred thousand employees in the public sector. Raymond Garneau's May 11 budget with stringent spending controls, sharply increased taxes on cigarettes for seven years to pay for the Olympics, and an 80 per cent increase in hospital insurance premiums was not a pre-election budget. The deficit was later expected to approach $900 million, or 41 per cent of the total deficit for all provinces in the 1976-77 fiscal year.

By the spring of 1976 the unpopularity of the government had
reached a new high and confidence in Premier Bourassa a new low. A
poll taken by the Centre for Public Opinion Research (CROP) indicated
that dissatisfaction with the government, which had risen from 35 to
54 per cent between October 1973 and November 1974, had risen to
66 per cent. Twenty-nine per cent believed René Lévesque best re-
sponded to the aspirations of the Quebeckers, almost double the 15
per cent who endorsed Bourassa. Asked how they would vote, their
intentions placed the PQ well in front. With the undecided distributed,
the results gave the Parti québécois a commanding lead of 41 per
cent to 28 per cent for the Liberals, a lead which was even more overwhelming among francophones and was even greater outside Montreal, where the west-end anglophone and ethnic opinion narrowed
the margin and where the minor parties were less influential. A Gallup
Poll taken early in May and published in *La Presse* on May 22 yielded
almost identical results with the PQ leading the Liberals 30.4 to 23 per
cent. Dissatisfaction had risen to 70 per cent, perhaps because the
government had passed Bill 23 in April preventing strikes by school
teachers. Of the 441 respondents who had voted Liberal in 1973 only
181 planned to do so again, while 67 had moved to the PQ and 130
were undecided.

	Lib	PQ	UN	Créd.	PNP	Other	?
Province of Quebec	21.5	31.6	7.6	6.9	9.8	4.1	18.6
Metropolitan Montreal	25.0	31.7	5.6	3.1	13.3	2.9	18.4
Metropolitan Quebec City	17.4	30.1	6.1	3.7	7.3	5.3	30.6
Rest of the province	18.7	31.7	9.9	11.5	6.3	5.2	16.7
French	17.7	35.4	7.9	7.9	9.3	3.9	17.8
English	37.3	12.2	4.7	1.6	14.0	4.7	25.6

Source: *La Presse,* April 22: ? includes don't know and refused to answer.

There was little to enhance the Liberal's popularity during the
spring and summer. The teachers refused to obey Bill 23 and continued mass walkouts, often joined by members of the common front.
And while at their April 25 convention the Liberals could applaud the
premier's promised tough stand against the common front of public
sector employees and his assurance that he would not give in to
blackmail, the public was generally outraged as one-day stoppages
hit schools and colleges, hydro services and hospitals. In July the Assembly was summoned to approve legislation ending a five-week
nurses strike, and by August the first stoppages heralded a province-
wide construction strike in September.

Moreover, non-francophone Montreal, important politically to the Liberals, was enraged with the government by the fall. The Protestant teachers were still without a contract, and struck on October 1. The English Canadians had never accepted the principle of Bill 22, which seemed to them to deny the equality of English and French and endanger anglophone schools, and had not been silenced by Chief Justices Deschênes' decision on April 6 that Bill 22 did not 'violate the constitutional guarantees of the British North America Act for that Act guaranteed religious not linguistic rights in education.' But the brunt of the real burden of Bill 22 was born by the children of immigrants, who had to demonstrate their proficiency in English or attend French schools. Parents threw their children into immersion courses, while the government and school boards faced the difficult task of devising reasonable testing methods. By the summer of 1976 the entire system was in disarray: families were broken up by the testing, several thousand cases were under appeal; parents were refusing to obey the instructions of the boards; and the principals of the anglophone schools in heavily Italian St Leonard directly challenged the government by admitting a thousand students who had failed the English-language test. On September 19 a crowd of fifteen hundred angry Italian, Greek, Portuguese, and Chinese parents met Premier Bourassa outside a Montreal hotel. He agreed to meet their spokesmen and promised that, if they would accept the principle of a lack of freedom of choice, he would ensure fairness and equity in the administration of the tests.

While Anglophones and new Canadians in Quebec threatened the strength of the Bourassa government in Quebec, their brethren outside seemed determined to give ammunition to the opponents of federalism. In December 1974 the federal government had announced that the use of French would gradually be extended at Quebec airports, but soon faced the opposition of the largely anglophone pilots' and controllers' associations, who argued that bilingual air-to-ground and cockpit communication was unsafe. The government first agreed to delay the extension of bilingualism and then, following a nine-day work stoppage by the pilots in June 1976 and enormous pressure from English Canada, agreed to a commission of inquiry. The commission was to report whether bilingualism could be implemented safely 'beyond a reasonable doubt' and the government would be bound by a free vote in the Commons. Meanwhile, regulations against the use of French were to be strictly enforced.

While the anglophone press applauded the agreement, and letters

"Of course he's dead. Would I be doing this
if he wasn't dead"?

Halifax *Chronicle-Herald*, May 13, 1976

to the editor revealed the extent of the backlash against bilingualism, the reaction in Quebec was explosive. Jean Marchand immediately resigned from the Trudeau cabinet, and other Liberal MPs threatened to leave the party. Industry Minister Guy Saint-Pierre admitted on August 14 that the English-Canadian response had led him to reconsider his attitude towards the separatist option. L'Association des Gens de l'Air du Quebec was formed by francophone pilots, controllers, and technicians and secured the legal services of Serge Joyal and Pierre de Bane, both Liberal MPs, to fight the regulations in the courts. The National Assembly unanimously passed a resolution of support, and the government donated $25,000 to help pay legal costs. Soon a committee of prominent Quebeckers from all parties and walks of life had been organized to arouse public opinion, and by the fall the symbol of linguistic pride, worn by such non-activists as Maurice Richard, was a lapel button which read 'Il y a du français dans l'air' '('there's French in the air'). When Toronto fans booed announcements in French during the September 7 Team Canada game with Sweden, every hockey fan in Quebec had a taste of the backlash.

The Parti québécois could have wished for nothing more. The events of the summer and fall, René Lévesque said on October 13, were a 'warning that the cup is full and that any attempt to impose more French will provoke a violent rejection from the English-speaking majority. Because that is plainly what is involved – from initial curiosity to resistance, English Canada is moving now to rejection. Without openly wishing that Quebec would leave, not going so far as to throw us out the door if we don't decide to go, it is certain that English Canada is no longer in the mood to tolerate either the smallest concession to Quebec or any acceleration of bilingualism in Canada.' The same day James Richardson resigned from the Trudeau cabinet to protest the possible entrenchment of French-language rights in a new constitution over which Quebec would have a veto. On October 18 – the day Bourassa was to call the Quebec election – the voters of Ottawa-Carleton clearly rejected the federal government's bilingual policy.

However inauspicious the outlook, the evidence of an approaching election was everywhere by the middle of September. The premier could repeat as late as September 20 that 'I see no reason that would justify calling an election at this time,' but within a week he was turning aside questions about an election with a smile. Acute observers

saw signs that the big red machine had been oiled, and cabinet ministers began discussing possible highway extensions, new hospital
wings, day-care centres, and the other benefits the electorate expects
at election time. It was difficult to find reasons to match the evidence.
The best that political observers could suggest was that the government hoped to cash in on post-Olympic euphoria and the backlash
against the public service unions, and perhaps anticipate any revival
of third-party strength.

Premier Bourassa later revealed that about the end of September
the Liberals had commissioned a Gallup Poll which indicated that the
Parti québécois was leading the Liberals 29.4 to 23.4 per cent. Both
the UN and Créditistes had gained strength since the spring with 12.2
per cent each, while the PNP secured 5.1 per cent. Only 20 per cent
were undecided or refused to answer. The poll also showed that only
45.3 per cent were in any way satisfied with the government's performance, and exactly half were dissatisfied with the premier personally. Nevertheless, according to rumours from Quebec City the Liberal
members were anxious for an election, while informed sources said
that at a meeting on September 29 the cabinet was split between
those who believed that conditions were too bad for an election and
those who believed they could only get worse.

The scenario became clear following the October 1-2 meeting of
the provincial premiers in Toronto when the provinces attempted to
create a consensus on constitutional change and patriation. On October 3, with posters screaming 'We Are Ready', the premier told Rivi-
ère-du-Loup Liberals that Mr Trudeau's threat to patriate the BNA Act
unilaterally was a threat to Quebec, and that the moment of truth was
at hand. At Sherbrooke on October 7 he observed solemnly that 'we
have a historic deadline to meet within the next few weeks or months'
and that the provincial conferences 'may be the only opportunity for
Quebec to define its place within a new Canadian federalism.' In what
was obviously an election speech he denounced the attempts of the
Péquistes to woo the anglophone as 'intellectual prostitution' and
dared the PQ to publish its manifesto: 'They are afraid because they
know I'll demolish them just as I demolished their budget for an independent Quebec during the 1973 campaign.'

The election campaign had begun. Any doubts were removed on
October 14 when the government suddenly made possible the end of
the Protestant teachers strike and on October 16 when the daily papers carried reassuring full-page ads 'THE BOURASSA TEAM IS WORKING
FOR YOU.'

'Stop separatism! Bourassa – only he can do it'

In his pre-recorded three-minute TV address on October 18, Premier Bourassa argued that he needed a mandate on two crucial issues: the form of a new constitution and a limitation on the right to strike in the public sector. 'In a very short time a number of very important events will effect the future of Quebec,' he said. 'These all involve discussions Quebec will have with its Canadian partners to determine its place in Canada. The upcoming discussions are the most important in a long time for our future. In order to associate all Quebeckers with this historical decision-making process which will result in the birth of a new Canada, I have decided to hold a general election November 15.' The public debate provided by an election, he continued, would allow Quebeckers to 're-evaluate the equilibrium of social groups within our society.' Some labour leaders, he observed, no longer wished 'to honour the special contract,' that is the right to strike in the public sector, agreed to in 1964. 'In fact, we have witnessed unacceptable abuses of the right to strike which have, on certain occasions, been equivalent to acts of cruelty with regard to defenceless persons. It has thus become essential to change the present situation. We pledge to do precisely that.' That the premier needed to define a constitutional position and develop a new approach to labour relations which would provide a little confidence and not provoke confrontation was unquestioned; that he needed a new mandate to do so was absurd.

During the campaign the Liberals did articulate a new position on constitutional reform, outlined a vague new approach to labour relations, and indicated their position and made promises on a wide range of other social and economic issues. The basic published campaign document was *Programme 76* unveiled by the premier on October 25 at a Montreal press conference. On the constitution the Liberals agreed to patriation providing a new constitution included: provincial legislative paramountcy in the field of arts and letters, with the right to opt out of any federal programme with fiscal compensation, legislative paramountcy in the field of communications, including cable television and the CBC; constitutional recognition of provincial paramountcy with regard to the integration and placement of immigrants, and provincial participation in recruitment and selection; provincial participation in Supreme Court appointments; provision that only in cases of national emergency could the federal government intervene in areas of provincial jurisdiction and only with provincial consent could Ottawa take over a provincial work by declaring it to be for the general advantage of Canada; a strict limitation on the federal spending power, and the provision that if federal funds were to be spent on matters coming within provincial jurisdiction the provinces would determine and establish the methods of allocation and would have the right to opt out; an amending formula that gave Quebec a veto; the responsibility of the federal government for removing regional disparities, promoting equality of income and opportunity for all Canadians, and continuing equalization and stabilization policies. There it was at last – cultural sovereignty and profitable federalism.

At the press conference Mr. Bourassa revealed that the recent meeting of provincial premiers had accepted much of the Quebec position (as a letter from Premier Lougheed to Prime Minister Trudeau on October 14 indicated). 'This was a breakthrough on a vital issue for Quebec,' he boasted. 'We need to have the support of the federal government but we are in a better position if we have these provinces and if we have a clear mandate from the people of Quebec on November 15.' Claude Ryan gave the Liberals a modest pat on the back. For those who still preferred the federalist option, he wrote in *Le Devoir* (October 26), 'even with those flaws of which it will never be completely free, the Liberals' recent move supplies much-needed reassurance at a time when we were beginning to wonder if that party was going to become a mere outpost of its federal big brother.'

Programme 76 stated that a general clean up in the labour field was an 'absolute priority.' While strikes would not be outlawed in the public sector they would be 'avoided' by changing the bargaining procedures to include such provisions as compulsory secret supervised strike votes, and if stoppages did occur essential services would be maintained. In the private sector strikes would be discouraged by the creation of a 'preventitive mediation service' which would find new methods of preventing conflicts or. 'at the very least, attenuate them by means of dialogue during the life of the agreement so as to enable the parties to meet under circumstances other than in strike or counterstrike situations.' Throughout the campaign striking hydro workers, who barred his way and attempted to interrupt his meetings, probably increased public sympathy for his appeal for a new mandate 'to get the unions into line.'

The platform also made the usual gesture to a wide range of economic and social policies. Economically the government promised to increase financial and technical assistance to small and medium-sized businesses; maintain a receptive policy to foreign investment; negotiate new regional development programmes with Ottawa; demand more forward linkages in the resource sector; improve rural and regional road systems; and exercise rigorous control over expenditure in the public sector. Socially, the promises included 1,500 new nursing units each year as well as improved health, leisure, transportation, and taxation benefits for the elderly; sixty thousand new homes a year for five years; increased family revenue support leading to a guaranteed family income; compulsory no-fault automobile insurance, and the partial deduction of real estate taxes from taxable income.

But far more indicative of the nature of the Bourassa campaign were the giant posters of himself under which the premier sat at the October 25 press conference: 'STOP SEPARATISM! BOURASSA – ONLY HE CAN DO IT. VOTE LIBERAL'. For all practical purposes the Liberal campaign was an attempt to turn the election into a referendum on separatism, a strategy that had worked so well in 1973. Under opposition pressure the Liberals were forced to defend their record and to outline their position on other issues, but nine-tenths of every Bourassa speech, and the public speeches and door to door canvassing of Liberal candidates, was devoted to raising the spectre of separatism. 'The Québécois want to settle the separatist threat once and for all, and this is the main thrust of our campaign,' said Bourassa in Richmond on October 31. Later that day he told an audience in L'Assomption: 'Our choice lies between a better standard of living, with social, economic and cultural progress , and the separatist adventure, the separatist threat.'

Without overstating the benefits of unreformed federalism, Bourassa warned that the $2.5 billion flowing from Ottawa for equalization payments and oil subsidies would be difficult to find in an independent Quebec. Some evidence that capital was leaving Quebec provided ammunition. On November 6 H.E. Wyatt of the Royal Bank admitted that there had been a modest movement of deposits, mostly from immigrants, out of Quebec since October 18, and that the transfers had become more active on November 5 when an opinion poll indicated that the Parti québécois was well in the lead. The next day in Joliette the premier warned his audience not to let the fox into the henhouse, and declared that the promised referendum would do nothing to reassure investors. On television a day later he wondered what would happen to the $800 million in Quebec savings bonds after a PQ victory. André Raynauld, who had resigned as chairman of the Economic

Council of Canada to run in Outremont, warned that it would take twenty-five years for the consequences of separatism to run their course, and estimated that all investment would be stalled even before the referendum and two-thirds of the construction workers in the private sector would be unemployed.

By early November it was clear that the attempt to make separatism the only issue was not succeeding. Having no alternative, the Liberal campaign simply seemed to run out of control. One of the premier's problems was that the Parti québécois refused to fight on the issue, and if possible refused even to mention it. During their two-hour October 24 radio debate, when most of the discussion was on labour relations, the economy, and the government's record, the premier had forced Lévesque to admit that he believed in independence and that if the first referendum did not succeed there would be another. But thereafter M. Lévesque refused to make any concrete statements on the economic consequences of independence. Premier Bourassa asked for another budget and mocked the PQ for refusing to publish its manifesto. How could a party deal with the enormous consequences of independence or even with the routine of government if it could not even run a newspaper, he asked, referring to the collapse of Le Jour. But the PQ refused to be drawn out.

Finally, on November 10 when Lévesque suggested that the fall in the value of the dollar was good for exports, the premier is reported to have exclaimed: 'I've got it. I'll challenge him to a public debate about what he just said. If he accepts I'll clobber him because he never could count, and if he refuses, he'll look bad. Either way I've got him.' During a radio address the next day M. Bourassa dared M. Lévesque, 'if he is not afraid,' to debate the economics of separatism and federalism. When there was no positive response the premier then dared his opponent to debate any and all subjects with him. For the next three days M. Lévesque's refusal, described as hypocritical and cowardly, was a major thrust of the premier's campaign. 'One wonders if they've decided to take up the feel for power instead of the feel for Quebec,' he asked contemptuously.

Finally in full page ads on Saturday, November 13, the Liberals delivered the last message:

'On Monday, we settle what our future is to be.
We mustn't fool ourselves.
We mustn't let anyone else fool us.
On Monday, it's not a simple choice between parties.

La Presse November 9, 1976

On Monday, an act whose full significance we will probably not have weighed could lose us one of the highest living standards in the world, destroy all we've built up, and take away all we've won.
On Monday, we must not trigger the separation process.
Really, our *choice* is *obvious*:
either we set Quebec adrift – towards inevitable *separation* from Canada. Their "referendum" is a gigantic election fraud, its results to be controlled as the Péquiste leaders rig that series of referendums in the same way their union allies have been rigging strike votes …
or else we vote for *the only party* that can give us *stability* and *security* while pledging itself to respond even better to the needs of all citizens.
It's either *one* or *the other*.
Think about it.
On Monday, let's not gamble everything we've won.
On Monday, let's not break up Canada.
Let's vote Liberal.'
The message was clear, but most observers did not believe that it had had the desired effect. Yet the premier was optimistic as he spent the last day of the campaign in the east end of Montreal. 'Everywhere we go we sense that voters have finally understood how critical and fraudulent a campaign the PQ has fought since the beginning where they refused to admit that they are in fact a separatist party,' he told some campaign workers. 'But we have managed to unmask them and show them for what they really are and I am sure that voters won't be duped when they go to the polling booths.'
Since the beginning of the campaign the premier had been saying, 'It's like a baseball game. 1970 was the first strike, 1973 was the second – and you can imagine what is going to happen on November 15. After the third strike, they will have to leave the game.' By the end of the campaign it was doubtful if Premier Bourassa had got the ball over the plate. Indeed, the Liberal campaign had been so ineffective that observers wondered if Bourassa had tried to throw balls rather than strikes. Claude Arpin wrote in the *Montreal Star* (November 13) that reporters following the premier had written an absurd scenario where Bourassa deliberately threw the election and then a year later, with the help of the Union nationale, crushed the referendum so devastatingly that the PQ was demolished. More realistically, however, many concluded that the Liberals must have been deliberately keeping a

low profile, and posing as potential losers to frighten the undecided and cautious to support them.

The Liberals acquired some power-hitters from Ottawa when Jean Marchand, Bryce Mackasey, and Roland Comtois left the Commons, and André Raynauld left the Economic Council, to enter provincial politics. Prime Minister Trudeau and the federal party refused to intervene, and although Marc Lalonde (who spoke of the dangers of independence on October 26) said that federal Liberals were free to campaign very few of them did so. As the Bourassa campaign faltered in November there were persistent rumours that Mr. Trudeau planned to speak out, until on November 10 his office felt compelled to issue a flat denial. On the other hand his comment that separatism was dead – repeated several times during the year – because the referendum tactic proved that the PQ knew that the Québécois would never endorse independence, did not lend credibility to the Liberal campaign. Asked on October 28 about the departure of the three MPs for Quebec he replied: 'I do not think they have gone because of any serious menace of separatism; but they wish to make sure that the government of Quebec is a strongly federalist government.' It was a strange comment, more a reflection on the federalist integrity of the Bourassa government than the dangers of the Péquistes.

While all four declared their commitment to federalism, only Roland Comtois, the veteran MP from Terrebonne, declared that he was back to do battle against the separatist menace. Facing Jacques Parizeau in L'Assomption, he declared 'I am a convinced anti-separatist and I'm just not ready to let this country break up. The best way to stop the separatists is to start right here in my riding, then I'm doing my part to stop them in the province.' André Raynauld said that what the province needed was 'clear and understood orientations and priorities,' but also told his constituents where he stood on a number of issues:

'Let's get down to basics. You are already aware of my deep convictions on the subject of Canadian federalism. Whether we want to or not, we cannot shut out the fact that the PQ is challenging Canada's existence, that it was founded to do so, and that it has attracted support that sees the independentist choice as basic. The PQ cannot be allowed to camouflage and conceal from the public the fact that independence is the mainspring of its existence. Those who, like myself, refuse to see Canada broken up, must not allow themselves to be duped into discussing everything but the basics; we mustn't waste our time quibbling about furniture arrangements when we no longer know whether there is going to be a roof over our heads.

'Canadian federalism is characterized by its adaptability to the dynamics of society and politics. So support for federalism and Canadian unity need not stop us from wanting Quebec City or Ottawa to hold more or less power. It is no betrayal of federalism to believe, as I do, that power must in principle be located as near the citizens as possible, giving them the chance to hold responsibility and participate fully in the decisions that concern them. What I favour, then, is a greater decentralization of powers – what I really want is a strong, autonomous Quebec in a united Canada.'

After several conversations with M. Bourassa, Jean Marchand decided to run in Louis-Hébert against the redoubtable Claude Morin. While his October 20 letter summarizing those discussions, released to the press by the premier a day later, underlined his commitment to federalism, it was to the Trudeau model, and the letter as a whole was a critical commentary on the Bourassa government rather than an anti-separatist manifesto.

'This letter is not intended as either an ultimatum or a claim to special status from one who will appear as a candidate in the coming Quebec election. I simply want to shed some light on points we have discussed together.

'And you will see how appropriate it is that, after more than 35 years of public life in the union movement and in politics, I should tell you officially where I stand and how I see the major problems facing the Québécois and Canadians generally.

'It is quite understood that I claim no right to anything that could change a party platform adopted by due process.

'First and foremost I am, as you have said, a federalist. In my own case, at least, this commitment does not stem from any more or less philosophical principles, but from my understanding of a geographical, economic, demographic and linguistic reality, a reality that it would be a delusion on our parts to plan to change in a radical way. Even if we can build up some system of protection against the encroaching tide in which we are floundering, it is Utopianism to imagine that a mere solemn statement such as a declaration of independence will have the slightest effect on the considerable forces bearing on our cultural and linguistic community from all sides.

'So we must find compromises, while at the same time making sure that we can in fact fulfil the great aims we have in view.

'I have read with interest the agreement among the ten provinces on the repatriation of the constitution and the division of powers between the federal and provincial governments. I note that, very likely for the first time, the provinces have managed a consensus. On the other hand, I note too the reply from the Prime Minister of Canada. My understanding is that a number of points in the text of the ten provinces are not fully clear and must soon be so, as they will have to be discussed with the federal government. You have indicated that I would be given an appropriate opportunity to convey my own opinion as to the problems raised, and begin discussion with you and your colleagues.

'I believe that you are in agreement with the bilingualism policy developed by the federal government. I see this as fundamental. I do not believe the country can function if the two official languages are not accepted and used as provided in the Official Languages Act ...

'I see it as a matter for regret that a morning paper should interpret Quebec's aim as the suppression of English-language rights. First, I find it hard to understand how this could be legally done, and in the second place I think it is the worst possible turn we could do the Québécois and the country. We ought to concentrate on expanding the use of French and not curtail the established rights of the other groups.

'The Anti-French campaign in some western provinces makes my hair stand on end, and I am surprised that there is not more opposition to these signs of group aberration.

'I am also in full sympathy with Quebec's aim of making French the working language in Quebec as quickly as possible. I know that industry is giving you strong co-operation in this area.

'I must, however, confess that the schooling regulations for the children of immigrants strike me as counter to the spirit of the kind of Canada we want to build. There can be no objection to any kind of incitement that may draw immigrants and their children into the French-speaking community, but I think there are other ways to success than the use of more or less coercive measures. You have indicated your interest in discussing this point with me. I hope we will find better guidelines than those now in force.

'You made reference in your election announcement to the attitude of certain union leaders. As you are aware, I spent 23 years of my life in the union movement. There is no question, then, of my turning anti-union. However, I do agree that we have seen some outrageous practices in this area. I note without pleasure that our traditional collective bargaining system has sometimes been perverted, particularly in the public and semi-public sectors. It was also agreed that we could discuss this important problem.

'In general, I agree with your broad objectives and am prepared to fight to see them realized. I recognize the importance of constitutional problems and provincial autonomy, but I believe that we must not underestimate the importance of the problems of inflation, prices, employment, economic development, etc.

'If a candidate whose opinions are those just expressed is acceptable to you, I am ready to offer myself under the Liberal banner. I would appreciate hearing from you as soon as possible.'

Although Mr Marchand continually emphasized the dangers of independence in his campaign, his reply to the question of what he would do if Quebec separated was not likely to cause nightmares: 'Well, as for me, I'm staying in Quebec City. I'm not changing my life one bit.'

The mercurial Bryce Mackasey, who had left the Trudeau cabinet during the September 14 shuffle, delivered a major, carefully prepared speech in Dorval on October 22. 'Do we have a future? Will it be enough ten years from now to be bilingual? Or will this province be virtually the confines of those whose mother tongue is French?' he asked his anglophone audience. Endorsing the principle that French must be the language of work in Quebec, he suggested that at work and at school the minorities were not being fairly treated. He then delivered his public letter to Premier Bourassa, whom he had seen earlier in the day: 'What are our responsibilities as Quebeckers during the next election? We can refuse to vote, a useless gesture. We can vote for separatism, an equally useless gesture. We can vote for other responsible parties dedicated to the preservation of federalism and a Quebec where there are no second class citizens. But if Prime Minister Bourassa happens to read my speech and *if* he were to say that some relief from Bill 22 will be forthcoming – perhaps along the lines I suggested – and spell out that relief; *if* we are assured of greater job opportunities in the public service; *if* we are offered the opportunity of increasing minority representation in the National Assembly or at least an opportunity of running for office; *if* we are offered an opportunity to help this province improve the quality of life of its citizens, help it to be ever-vigilant against assimilation; if we are assured that in a reasonable period of time both official languages will be taught by competent teachers in all our schools; if progress is made to bring the Constitution home and to enshrine therein rights of the minorities – what then will be our excuse for turning our back if called upon to serve. Some have met the challenge but too few in number. They need help. If the next government gets elected without your support, then the extremists can say 'who needs them?' And slowly but surely we and all Canadians will be on the road to two solitudes. This time for good.'

Mackasey undoubtedly gave the Liberals strength in Montreal's west end, where some believed they could be in serious trouble. Possibly the Mackasey-Marchand criticism of the administration of the language provisions of Bill 22 – Mackasey personally supported the PQ position that all present immigrants should have freedom of choice and all future immigrants should have none – helped to persuade the government to relax the regulations, although the premier argued that the decision was the result of an official report and was not politically motivated. On November 2 the premier and Education Minister Jean Bienvenue announced that linguistic proficiency could be determined by interviews rather than tests, children with siblings in anglophone schools would have freedom of choice, and English would be compulsory in francophone schools in grade three. Like so much of what Claude Ryan called the policy of 'zigzag', the changes pleased no one. Angelo Montini, president of the Italian Canadian Education Council, denounced it all as one 'election bluff' and warned the Liberals not to expect the Italian vote. A francophone audience at Thetford Mines booed the premier's statement that English would be taught in grade three. As anglophone candidates in Montreal continued to attack the principle of the educational provisions of Bill 22 – George Springate even demanding that Bourassa promise changes in the act or 'throw me out' – a harassed and frustrated premier finally replied: 'We are against free choice in the language of teaching. Those who do not agree with us should leave.'

The November 2 announcement was also seen as a result of pressure from Ottawa. Indeed to Claude Ryan the 1976 descent on Quebec was seen as '1965 in reverse' when the Marchand-Pelletier-Trudeau team went to Ottawa to save the country from Quebec nationalism. But he also saw it as a comment on the Bourassa government:

'Mr. Bourassa undoubtedly thinks he has made a fine catch by signing up these three gentlemen. If he is willing to listen to what they have been telling him, he must admit that their decisions are not unrelated to the weakness of his own leadership. The most striking thing about the motives of Messrs Marchand, Mackasey and Raynauld is, first and foremost, their ill-concealed concern about the perils to which the country is exposed by an irresolute, indecisive government. This has been generally reported for months. We now have it confirmed in the most meaningful possible way.

'No doubt, some significant tactical reasons underlie the decisions of all the federal personalities entering the provincial lists. Mr. Macka-sey, for example, will be bait to regain the confidence of the English-speaking voters. M. Marchand can make the most of his battle for the rights of the Gens de l'Air; Mr. Raynauld can stress his long experience in public administration and economic affairs. It must also be agreed that, independently of any other consideration, each man had the absolute right to the decision he made. Given the striking parallels between their reasons, however, their decisions can be understood as dictated largely by the scant confidence inspired in Ottawa by the Quebec Liberal Party's current drift and the leadership of M. Bourassa' (*Le Devoir*, October 22).

Claude Morin drew more laughs during a joint meeting with Jean Marchand on November 1: 'C'est le Front des Libéraux d'Ottawa pani-qués – le FLOP.' In many ways it was a flop, as Marchand and Comtois were soundly defeated and André Raynauld barely hung on in the solidly Liberal Outremont.

The Parti québécois

Circumstances could hardly have been better for René Lévesque and the Parti québécois. For a year the Liberals had seemed unable to come to grips with the economic problems of the province or relax the social tensions that accompanied labour unrest and cultural controversy. The minor parties had neither fused, nor had become perceived as a possible alternative to the Liberals. The Péquistes had continually improved their regional and local organizations, however, and in May completed a $1,200,000 fund-raising drive which was to enable them to match the saturation media exposure of the Liberals. Moreover, since 1973 the Parti québécois had continued to soften its image and that of its leader.

The party programme, described by Lévesque as social democratic, remained the same on social and economic policy as in 1973. While it called for more public control (if not ownership), restrictions on foreign investment, and the development of a national plan by representatives of labour, industry, and the state, the party remained

committed to a mixed economy. Moreover, while there were many ul-
tra-socialists in the party the leadership had attempted to neutralize
the most outspoken and, according to Dominique Clift (*Montreal Star*,
May 15), local conventions for the selection of candidates were 'being
manipulated to push aside all persons who are too closely identified
with left-wing labor tendencies, with extreme anti-business attitudes,
and with glaring cultural jingoism.'

By 1976 the image had been softened on the independence question as well. Before the 1973 election the party had promised a referendum before negotiating independence, but the promise came late
in the campaign and was extremely vague. The issue had been the
source of intense conflict within the party in 1974 and 1975, but the
electoral wing – or the 'power before principle' element as their opponents put it – won. By the summer of 1976 Lévesque outlined the procedure for the readers of *Foreign Affairs* (July): 'Let us suppose it
does happen, and Québec peacefully elects such a government.
What then?

'The way we see it, it would have to go somewhat like this. There is
a new Québec government which is totally dedicated to political independence. But this same Québec, for the time being, is still very much
a component of federal Canada, with its quite legitimate body of elected representatives in Ottawa. This calls, first of all, for at least a try at
negotiation. But fruitful talk between two equally legitimate and diametrically opposed levels of government, without any further pressure
from the population – that would be a real first in Canadian political
history! Obviously, there would have to be the referendum which the
Parti québécois proposed in order to get the decisive yes-or-no answer to the tired question: What *does* Québec want ? (This was precisely the procedure by which the only new province to join Confederation during our recent democratic past, Newfoundland, was
consulted in 1948-49 about whether or not to opt in. So why not about
opting out?) If the answer should be no, then there's nothing to do but
wait for the momentum of change to keep on working until the answer
is yes, oui, then the pressure is on Ottawa, along with a rather dramatic surge of outside attention, and we all get a privileged opportunity to study the recently inked Helsinki Declaration and other noble
documents about self-determination for all peoples.

'Fully confident of the basic integrity of Canadian democracy, and
just as conscious that any silliness would be very costly for both sides,
we firmly believe that the matter would then be brought to a negotiated settlement.'

The party brochure, *2 ou 3 choses à propos de l'indépendance*, answered the question whether it was possible for a PQ government to declare independence suddenly and unilaterally as follows: 'No, that is quite out of the question. The Parti québécois sees two situations as possible following its election. Either the transfer of powers and resources from Ottawa to Quebec occurs according to a schedule established jointly with Ottawa; in this case independence is not realized suddenly or unilaterally. Or else Ottawa stands in the way of the transfer; in this case the Quebec government reports on the state of discussions to the Québécois population, and asks them to decide by referendum, in the light of the facts, whether they want to continue with the accession to sovereignty.' Neither the brochure nor Lévesque denied that every effort would be made to negotiate a transfer of powers without a referendum, and both were silent on clause one of the platform adopted in 1974 which called for the immediate enactment of legislation authorizing the government to negotiate independence with Ottawa.

By the beginning of 1976 the party had adopted its election posture and strategy. As Lévesque told the Quebec regional Péquiste congress on March 6 – and repeated endlessly at party meetings – the party must think of itself as 'the government party' with 'concrete preoccupations and an ability to act efficiently and realistically.' The party executive, he explained, was currently preparing a working paper on the priorities of a PQ government which it would submit to the party congress late in 1976 or early in 1977, but which it would use, after approval by the national council, if an election was held earlier. At regional meetings across the province Lévesque appealed for concentration on organizing for the expected fall election, not on ideological debate, and urged party discipline rather than the open warfare that had so often characterized the PQ in the past. Lévesque himself believed that the party had reached what he described as a new maturity and acquired a sense of prudence as the Bourassa government became increasingly unpopular and the PQ was clearly the only alternative.

But the ideological swing to the centre, the softer image, and the concentration on the struggle for power generated tensions within the party that not even the possibility of victory could still. As one disgruntled Péquiste told a sympathetic Lysiane Gagnon (*La Presse*, September 18), 'If we keep compromising now, what will it be like when we're in office?' The most visible sign of the tension was the conflict between the leaders of the party and the staff of *Le Jour*. When the paper had been established in 1974 by Lévesque, Jacques Parizeau, and Yves Michaud, management controlled the editorial page, but the reporters were given control over the rest. Although the PQ owned only 5 per cent of the shares, *Le Jour* was widely regarded as a paper which reflected party opinion. Yet as the party swung to the right the paper moved to the left; as the party attempted to become less partisan and intolerant the paper became more militant and abrasive. A front-page editorial on May 1 accused the PQ of ceasing to be a workers party and argued that in an independent Quebec there would have to be a new party to represent the social democratic views of the working class. Another on May 8, entitled 'The common front – our struggle' and signed by *Le Jour* workers union, supported the common front of public service employees in its dispute with the government as part of a legitimate class struggle, at a time when Lévesque was attempting to keep the radical trade unions at arms length.

The paper's financial crisis provided the opportunity for intervention. Although *Le Jour* had achieved a circulation of about thirty thousand, the same as *Le Devoir*, it had lost over $450,000 since its inception, and was losing about $45,000 a month in 1976, partly because neither the federal nor provincial governments bought advertising. On May 29 the national executive elected representatives to meet with the shareholders of *Le Jour* and formally instructed them to express 'the dissatisfaction of the executive with the contents of the paper and its ideological approach over the past months,' state clearly that the party would not continue to support the paper if it maintained 'its style and present orientation,' and demand that the control of the newspaper be changed. The meeting was held on May 3, when Bernard Landry, spokesman for the executive, said that 'some people consider that the Parti québécois is a hostage of *Le Jour*, but the hostage is fed up with being in jail and intends to get out even if it has to smash the door down.' As the shareholders applauded, the *Le Jour* journalists left the meeting. Speaking for the board, Jacques Parizeau explained that the paper would have to raise $200,000 and cut staff and other expenses to remain alive. *Le Jour* did not publish on June 1, as the reporters walked out, and later that day Robert Burns, the left-wing MNA, charged that management not the journalists was responsible for the crisis. Claude Charron, another radical MNA, added that cuts must not include the reporters, while others criticized the executive for interfering with freedom of the press.

Lévesque replied angrily on June 3 through the press (*Le Devoir*, June 4), publishing the resolution and observing that Robert Burns, who had not bothered to attend the May 29 meeting, did not speak for the executive. Lévesque then observed: '*Le Jour* was founded by independentists and supported with equal loyalty and generosity by thousands of Parti québécois members and sympathizers – and to a modest extent, out of the budget of the party itself – in the hope of having, not a slavish echo of "the machine," but a vigorous, informed, and balanced expression of our choice.

'Now, for a good while our distinct impression has been that the portion of the paper self-managed by a group of staff members was not gratifying this hope. Sometimes, in fact, this portion seems to promote even in news items, a thinking which is clearly contrary to the broad objectives outlined in *Le Jour's* charter. In public opinion, as well as among numerous independentists for whom *Le Jour* is still connected with the Parti québécois, this gives rise to increasing confusion and concern. Having scrupulously avoided all interference in this area from the beginning, the Executive Council then had the right and the duty as a minority shareholder to make it known that the party had no intention of being made hostage to such misrepresentation. So it was not the freedom of the press at stake in this case, but the freedom of the Parti québécois.'

At a meeting of the executive and the parliamentary wing on June 9 in a Quebec City hotel, the decision was made not only to withdraw support of *Le Jour*, but on a 10-to-4 vote, with three abstentions, to prevent anyone connected with *Le Jour* running as a candidate or belonging to the national executive. (Lévesque, Jacques-Yvan Morin, and Marc-André Bédard apparently voted against the last part of the resolution.) At the national council meeting at Joliette on June 19-20, however, Jacques Parizeau succeeded in having the provision overruled, but the council approved cutting the link with the paper. On August 10 the shareholders gave management full powers over the paper, and the journalists withheld their by-lines and used a front-page editorial to accuse management of political censorship. The paper died on August 25 as the dispute led to the lockout of the staff and was formally buried on September 23. 'Infiltration, agitation and suicidal radicalism killed *Le Jour*,' observed Jacques Parizeau, for the reporters believed that 'the sabotage of what is progressive is another step towards the great night of the revolution.' To which they replied: 'The adventure of *Le Jour* is of capital importance in the understanding of the future leaders of Quebec.' The radicals were more outspoken in their criticism of Lévesque's leadership, and Claude Charron said that the party needed a 'detonator.'

But at the national council meetings at Joliette in June and Shawinigan on October 2-3 the cracks were at least papered over, and attention was focused on the coming campaign. Camille Laurin told the Joliette meeting that the emphasis over the summer was to be on deeper penetration in the rural and semi-rural areas to give the party a real presence throughout the province, and that following a policy of decentralization the regional and local budgets had been increased from $300,000 to $500,000. (The council was also told that the party would create a permanent policy commission which would examine all proposed legislation before a PQ government introduced it in the Assembly, and if it was not faithful to the party platform would call a meeting between the government and the party, and if necessary call a national convention, to resolve the differences.) At Shawinigan, Lévesque stated that an election would be announced within three weeks and appealed 'urgently to everyone to get to work with a will, for a few weeks, calmly and with discipline, so that we can carry off the victory.' Apparently to avoid arousing any further tension, the party decided not to present the manifesto and/or the list of post-victory legislative priorities.

The election strategy had been determined well before Bourassa called the election on October 18. The campaign would be fought on the record of the Bourassa government and the existence of the PQ as the only alternative. The promise of a referendum would defuse the question of independence, and allow non-separatist Quebeckers to vote Péquiste. Little would be said of the PQ platform, and Bourassa would be given nothing to attack as he had been with the catastrophic presentation of the PQ budget in 1973. Above all, the election would be fought on the local level – riding by riding. The model was that of Daniel Johnson in 1966 when the Liberals had won the province but lost in the ridings. With one million dollars in party funds, one million from the government, and one million to be collected, the PQ chest was sufficiently full to permit adequate local and provincial media exposure.

PQ campaign literature was carefully designed to focus attention on the Bourassa government. Posters trumpeted 'Ça ne peut plus continuer comme ça.' Hand-outs featured a picture of Bourassa with the caption 'On merite mieux que ça' – better than the Olympic debt and

James Bay, increased taxes and enormous deficits, inflation and un-employment, labour unrest and social tension, inadequate housing and high automobile insurance, land speculation and lack of support for farmers, and provincial impotence in the face of federal aggres-sion. The English-language brochure was entitled *Enough is Enough*: enough of a government tainted by scandal and addicted to patron-age, enough of a government whose educational language policy pleased no one. The Parti québécois, the party of the Québécois, would provide 'a real government', and a wise and distinguished look-ing Lévesque was 'a real leader.' The Lévesque team was 'The Que-bec team at the service of Québécois,' the only real alternative to an-other four years of M. Bourassa. The team was remarkably strong, although educators were about as over-represented as lawyers were in traditional parties. The party was strengthened enormously at the popular level by the addition of Lise Payette, the best known of Quebec's TV personalities. The entry of Rodrigue Tremblay, chairman of the University of Montreal's economic department, helped to calm the fearful. On November 2 he assured the Economists Association of Quebec that the number one priority of a PQ government would be economic growth, and that new social programmes would have to wait. Looking over the list of PQ candidates no voter could deny that there was the quality and experience to form a government.

Opening the PQ campaign on October 20, M. Lévesque predicted that he had a 50-50 chance of forming a government. 'Rigorously scientific' polling by the party in forty-five key ridings during the past year, he stated, revealed that the Péquistes had a chance in all ridings but those in the anglophone west end of Montreal and a few others throughout the province and could win as many as one hundred seats. He told a press conference that he would concentrate on urg-ing the voters to throw out the 'corrupt and morally bankrupt' Bour-assa regime. Reaffirming his commitment to independence, he de-clared that the separatist option was not an issue in the election. 'We have already accepted a solemn undertaking to hold a referendum on the issue and that will be the time to talk about independence.' Later, in an interview with the *Montreal Star* (November 5) Lévesque de-clared that the party 'if elected would feel it had a mandate to start ne-gotiations with Ottawa with a view to sovereignty.' But he added, 'there is not a snowball's chance in hell that the federal government would agree to give us back full powers.' There would therefore have to be a referendum, with one clearly understood question, probably

within two years. 'If we win, no one in Canada or Quebec will be able
to say that we don't have a mandate to negotiate out of Canada.' The
referendum was 'a bet we are making on Canada's integrity,' he said.
'It has a lot to lose by not respecting the will of the French Canadian
people.' Once Ottawa agreed to negotiate – before or after a referendum – a civilized timetable would be drawn up for the transition: 'It
may take two to three years, once the process is started and during
that time we could have two or three referendums.'

Although Lévesque kept a watchful eye on his own riding of Taillon,
he blanketed the province by car, helicopter, and plane and visited
some critical areas two or three times – such as Lac St Jean. Even in
Liberal bastions the reception was enthusiastic, and a devoted press
gave him maximum and almost uncritical news coverage. While the
tone and content sometimes differed, there was a basic sameness to
his speeches. Everywhere Bourassa was awarded the Triple Crown
for high taxes, unemployment, and deficits. The costs of the Olympics
– which he would recover from Ottawa – and of James Bay were
never neglected. Nor were scandals – 'I'm not a scandal sheet. The
whole government is a scandal. It's not criminality so much as it is a
lack of morality.' Jean Marchand's arrival – 'a thinly disguised putsch
by the federal Liberals to take over the 'branch plant' government in
Quebec – provided ample opportunity to attack Mr. Trudeau and to
underline the failure of biculturalism and bilingualism. Under Mr. Tru-.
deau and friends, he told his constituents on October 21, two solitudes had become 'two hostilities.' The anti-French backlash was kill-
ing bilingualism, he argued, and with mock sorrow in his voice –
'because I knew them' – Trudeau and Marchand have 'unwittingly
been putting us in a straitjacket and building for themselves careers
as traitors to their own people.' Premier Bourassa accepted
Marchand's conditions, he added, because 'the real power in the Liberal party, the money, is in Ottawa.' Jean Marchand was ridiculed for
'finding a new virginity as a Quebec nationalist after having tolerated
for three years as federal transport minister the restrictions on the use
of French in air communications which he now denounced.' Why
were there no francophone pilots in the $75,000-a-year bracket flying
jumbos? he asked. Because Air Canada insists that they live in Toronto – 'for security reasons no doubt.'

At the same time the Parti québécois hoped to attract some anglophone votes, or perhaps persuade some to stay home. On October 25
he told the Montreal Canadian Club that Bill 22 was unjust and inhu-

RENE
LEVESQUE
un vrai chef

c'est
le temps
de l'union
nationale

Non aux séparatistes!
Bourassa notre garantie
Votons Libéral

ON MERITE
MIEUX QUE ÇA

man but that, while his government would allow freedom of choice, all future immigrants, including the anglophone, would have to be educated in French. Then he appealed to his largely anglophone audience to join a free Quebec. 'You are Quebeckers, just as we are – although you may not have the same national stirrings as French-speaking Quebeckers – try to understand what is going on. Whether you are for it, or against it, take part in it.' Independence was inevitable, he told the overflow audience, for 'once the idea of national identity is rooted, it cannot be arrested.' On November 4 *Enough is Enough* was released at a press conference attended by the PQ candidates from all Montreal ridings with a significant anglophone and ethnic vote.

A major tactical concern were the relations between the party and organized labour. While the Parti québécois wanted to capitalize on labour unrest, it realized that too strong a pro-labour stance would lose votes. While Lévesque denounced Bourassa's labour policy, the PQ offered only vague expressions of good will such as the promises to change the labour code to better guarantee the rights of workers and union democracy and to restore confidence in the public sector by negotiating in good faith. While blaming the government for the Hydro strike, he appealed to the workers to provide necessary services and argued that society could not tolerate strikes in essential services.

Moreover, a more positive stance was unnecessary. Both the Confederation of National Trade Unions and the teachers union had denounced the Liberal government, and their élites at least were openly Péquiste. On October 25 Louis Laberge declared that his 275,000-member Quebec Federation of Labour would support the PQ because the party was the most worker-oriented and democratic. Asked if he was a separatist the fiery Laberge replied: 'I am a Québécois and I am in favour of telling the federal government to mind its own business and leave Quebec's business alone. I am a Québécois living in a country called Canada. But don't call me a federalist either.' What could be clearer?

On November 3 Laberge told a press conference that the response to the call to support the PQ had been amazing. Several hundred unionists were working as PQ organizers, he declared, and after meetings with union leaders across the province it was clear that the Liberals would get very few QFL votes. He also released copies of a special issue of *Le Monde Ouvrier* spelling out union dissent with the government, over one hundred thousand of which were to be distributed during the next week when workers throughout Quebec were to hold special 'membership meetings' to discuss the QFL's stand against the Liberal party.

The Lévesque campaign was not totally negative, however. Beginning late in October he outlined PQ policies on specific subjects in a very general way. At Chicoutimi on October 27 he promised to introduce compulsory and universal no-fault automobile insurance. A day later at Rimouski he promised a $50-million extension of the medicare programme which could be paid for out of existing premiums, for the recent increase in premiums 'are not being used for health care but rather to finance extravagant schemes like the Olympics.' A new housing policy was unveiled at Hull on October 31 when Lévesque promised to build seven thousand subsidized houses a year and control land speculation by passing a law taxing speculative gains similar to Ontario's. The municipalities received their good news in Valleyfield on November 3 when Lévesque promised to index and make statutory financial grants to municipalities, reform the municipal tax structure, and, in time, increase municipal revenues by $200 million.

The farmers were given a $50 million aid programme in Rimouski on November 8. 'A baneful, evil federal system' was to blame for the decline of Quebec's share of national agricultural income from 15 to 9.9 per cent between 1970 and 1975, he declared, and 'federal agriculture policy is at its most brutal and discriminatory in Quebec, especially for the milk producers of the province who have lost forty million dollars in income.' A PQ government would protect agricultural land, provide subsidies and credits, and increase consumption through such programmes as free school milk. At Sherbrooke on November 9 the small businessman was told that the government would direct the $2.5 billion in government purchases to small and medium-sized Quebec businesses. He also promised to provide technical and financial aid to small business.

When Lévesque wound up his campaign in the kitchens of Taillon it was clear that it had gone exactly as planned. The low profile, the absence of monster rallies, the small entourage had all been planned. Indeed, during the last week there were no public meetings at all, as Lévesque travelled about the province meeting local élites, talking to journalists, answering questions on hot-line shows, and generating masses of copy. Unlike 1973, in 1976 Premier Bourassa had been

given nothing to shoot at, and Lévesque had sounded convincing that
the question of independence could be put off to another day.

They also ran

The Quebec voter had no lack of alternatives on November 15. The
Union nationale, under new management, was determined to recover
from its sad 1973 fate. Jerome Choquette was confident his Parti national populaire had a future. The Créditistes continued to live on past
glories and present illusions. The New Democratic party refused to be
counted out. And the Democratic Alliance appeared in the English ridings in Montreal.

The Democratic Alliance was formed in the summer of 1976 by Nick
auf der Maur, a Montreal city councillor and one of the founders of the
Montreal Citizens Movement. The Alliance sought the support of
those who opposed Bill 22 and wanted freedom of choice, but could
not support the PQ. The Alliance attracted the support of many social
activists who were members of the New Democratic party and it was
attacked by the Quebec leader of the NDP, Henri Gautrin, who announced that the NDP and the Regroupement des militants syndicaux,
headed by Jacques Beaudoin of the Transport Union, had united and
planned to run thirty candidates in the election. By November 15 the
Alliance had nominated 12 candidates and the NDP-RMS 21.

The Créditistes seemed to have lost even the momentum that had
given them almost 10 per cent of the popular vote in 1973. At the May
1-2 congress the party had become more nationalistic with resolutions demanding a special status for Quebec that would give the province full control over credit, direct taxes, commerce, immigration, and
communications. With 108 candidates in the field Camille Samson
boasted that this party would win forty seats with strong showings in
Abitibi, the eastern townships, and Montreal. The Union nationale, he
argued, was a spent force, and the Créditistes would pick up the anti-
Bourassa non-separatist vote. Although M. Samson campaigned in
various parts of the province and planned to spend about $200,000 on
radio and television, the party seemed to count on a visit-and-tele-
phone chain letter to become the third force. But for the nostalgic
there was still a little of the old Socred touch when Samson told about
thirty of the faithful at Cap-de-la-Madeleine on November 7 that the
leaders of the Parti québécois, the trade unions, and Hydro Quebec
were all communists.

At the beginning of the year a real third force seemed possible with the apparent willingness of Jerome Choquette, who had resigned from the Bourassa cabinet in 1975 and formed the Parti national populaire, and Maurice Bellemare, temporary leader of the Union nationale, to discuss a merger. Rodrigue Biron, elected leader of the UN in May 1976, also apparently supported the idea of a merger, and on August 4 Biron and Choquette informed the press that the two parties had agreed to a joint committee to plan a merger. But before the day was over spokesmen for the UN had denied that Choquette was the senior in the alliance or that there would be a leadership convention in 1977. M. Choquette's statement on August 6 that he now believed in freedom of language choice in education – a complete reversal of his position as minister of education in the Bourassa cabinet – made the alliance an absurdity. Biron announced on September 3 that the dalliance was over.

The PNP was Jerome Choquette, although he had been joined in 1975 by Fabien Roy, the dissident Créditiste. Late in 1975 a poll had indicated that of the one in three Quebeckers who supported the idea of a new party – a third force – 27 per cent favoured Choquette as leader. But by the spring various polls gave the PNP from 9.8 to 4 per cent of the vote. On October 20 the PNP leader, whose position was to be confirmed four days later at the founding convention in Quebec city, journeyed to the Ottawa press gallery to make his manifesto public. His position was uncompromisingly federalist: 'I am for a strengthened federal connection. By this I mean the determination never again to challenge the destiny of the Canadian union, guarantor of a prosperous Quebec. Quebec's own interests make this imperative. Without the federal guarantee, Quebec would sink among the reefs of chance. With its exit from Confederation Quebec would suddenly be without investments and markets. Who would buy its surplus products? Where would it find the capital necessary for healthy industry and employment? Canada would barricade itself behind a system of prohibitive customs duties. From this viewpoint federalism is not only profitable but absolutely essential if we are to have a political existence. Abandonment of federalism would make Quebec a member of the club of the poor nations of the world. It can keep its wealth only by maintaining the Canadian federation, the only acceptable option that gives us the essentials along with the non-essentials. Everything else is simply a literary exercise, the blackest of all being separatism.'

Turning to provincial affairs, he declared that he intended 'to develop the inter-community front, in other words the alliance of Quebec's two peoples, and for three reasons: first, to prevent the language clash from degenerating into a race war; then, to block the separatist adventure; and finally, to assemble that third force which will come from the union of the two silent majorities of the two peoples, and prevent the weak opportunism that has been established as a system of government from extorting a fresh mandate. This alliance of Quebec's two nations is essential, but impossible without the repeal of Bill 22. Free choice of the language of instruction, a freedom likely to reinforce civil order, is made imperative by the many-sided complexity of Montreal in particular.

'Bill 22 leads to separatism. So that M. Bourassa's Liberal party, by their legislation, and M. Lévesque's Péquistes, by their doctrine, are locking Quebec into a dilemma. Both end in separatism. The PNP offers Quebec an alternative that can free it from this dilemma. It opposes the separatist opposition, a dead end, with the choice of Canadian Liberalism within the framework of the federation that serves our interests and is essential to Quebec's survival. Separatism is a suicide leading to the economic demise of the French-Canadian nation.'

The PNP represented the alternative 'to statism, syndicalism and separatism, the three myths of the quiet revolution.' The PNP state would be based on pure economic liberalism where the individual was freed of heavy taxes, the state of large expenditures, and society of strikes. Despite Mr Choquette's reputation the PNP never really materialized. Thirty-seven candidates were nominated, but the press, even in Montreal, paid only lip service to the party and it was not a serious element in the campaign.

As the popularity of the Bourassa government waned, the Union nationale seemed to come to life. Reduced to 5 per cent of the popular vote in 1973 and with only Maurice Bellemare in the Assembly (from a 1974 by-election), the party faced a massive task of reconstruction. At the May 22-23 convention the delegates entrusted the task to Rodrigue Biron when they elected him to the leadership on the first ballot, well ahead of four other equally unknown candidates. The forty-one-year-old Biron, a Laval commerce graduate, managed the family foundry at Sainte-Croix de-Lotbinière and had been mayor of that town. A Liberal until he announced his candidacy in March, Biron had a good campaign style and seemed to attract the young men in three-piece suits whom reporters had seen working for Brian Mulroney in the federal Conservative leadership convention.

Within a few weeks M. Biron had reorganized the general staff and developed an electoral strategy. The intention was to concentrate heavily on organizing only about thirty-five ridings. Dr William Shaw of Pointe Claire, a candidate for the leadership, was placed in charge of Montreal anglophone ridings, where anglophones would be nominated as they would in other English ridings in the province. By October 1 Biron and his associates had 127 resolutions on policy ready for a party conference attended by 1,624 delegates. The general thrust of the resolutions was towards massive decentralization of services and decision-making, aid to the small businessman, the farmer, and the family. The right to strike would be abolished in the public sector and replaced by mechanisms for negotiation, conciliation, and arbitration. Strikes were allowed in the private sector only if approved by an absolute majority in a secret ballot.

The most controversial resolutions concerned language. In 1973 the party had promised that French would be the only official language and that children of all future immigrants would be educated in French schools. However, after lengthy debate the party relaxed its position and decided that only the children of non-anglophone immigrants would be compelled to attend French schools. In addition, while French would be the national language, both French and English would be recognized as official languages. On the constitution the party deserted such slogans as 'equality or independence' and did not attempt to find middle ground between the Liberals and the separatists. The resolutions were remarkably similar to the Liberal platform released on October 25 as the party recommended a 'global revision' of the constitution which would give the member states control over the Supreme Court, limit the federal government's spending power, and give the member states control over education, health, social security, communications, and cultural affairs and responsibility for establishing the priorities and administering programmes in immigration, regional development, and housing.

Claude Ryan of *Le Devoir* (October 4) found the congress heartening. The social and economic policy resolutions, like the members of the UN, were generally practical, if vague. With the linguistic and constitutional resolutions, he commented, the party had 'aligned itself with some recent manifestations of Québécois nationalism that show greater involvement in bread-and-butter issues and retain a connection with the old Quebec tradition of equality in language rights.' With the efforts of the last few months, he concluded, the UN 'is getting back into the race.' 'Though it hasn't yet found a truly province-wide dimension, it is making progress in terms both of the men leading it and of the ideas it has to offer. In the coming election, given a little organization, it could produce some surprises in at least a few regions where people are dissatisfied with the Liberals, though not taken with either the PQ or the Créditistes, and have not completely forgotten their own not too distant past.'

With only about $400,000 in party funds and a rapidly created organization M. Biron, the only bearded party leader in Canada, led what he described as his 'new army' into what could be its last battle. Although he faced strong Créditiste opposition in his own riding of Lotbinière, Biron was constantly on the road. Like the Parti québécois, Biron planned to win on the local level by constantly hammering at the Bourassa government and underlining local grievances. He did draw on the party resolutions, however, to make promises concerning aid to farmers and small businesses, more housing, improved Metro transportation, a guaranteed annual income, abolition of school taxes, and the control of labour. Seldom referring to the Parti québécois, he was eager to denounce the hidden separatists of the Liberal party.

Winding up his campaign in Quebec on November 14 he warned that a Liberal victory would trigger an even more explosive social climate in the province. There was no doubt that the bulk of the people agreed that the government had to be defeated, he argued, and if it was returned because of the fear of separatism Quebec's problems would be settled on the street. To the suggestion that Quebec had to suffer the shortcomings of the government or the consequences of separatism the UN replied in full page ads on November 13:

'What nonsense. What arrogance. Because there IS a choice, a FEDERALIST choice, represented by a new and reconstructed Union Nationale Party which has been revitalized by disillusioned Liberals, Progressive Conservatives, Créditistes and the traditional bleus from the rural areas. We are Canadians and Quebeckers and we stand foursquare for Federalism and the preservation of Canada.

'You, the Electorate, are intelligent people and we know the Liberals will no longer be able to resort to intimidation and panic tactics in order to gain your support.'

The Biron and UN campaign had been quite extraordinary. Not only did the party reveal a new sense of purpose, indeed of urgency, but it secured an amazingly good press. While the press noted that the solutions were vague and Biron's speeches neither deep nor profound, the reporters were more than willing to give full play to his attacks on the Bourassa government. By November 15 it was clear that the party had a reasonable chance in about twenty ridings and could influence the outcome in another twenty.

Portents and prophecies

Viewed from the top there had been three or four quite distinct and almost unrelated campaigns. None of the parties accepted the Premier's invitation to fight the battle on the issue of independence, and the real election was fought in the ridings. There was not one election, as in 1973, but 110. If there was an issue common to all ridings it was the record of the premier and his government. A poll in early November indicated that 41 per cent believed that management of the economy was the most important issue, and 30 per cent placed it second. Honesty in government was ranked first by 12 per cent, and second by 18. A poor fourth was independence with only 7 and 8 per cent placing it first and second. Ultimately, local questions – milk quotas, strikes, unemployment – and provincial issues focused on a single point – satisfaction with the Bourassa government. The same poll revealed that 67 per cent of those responding were dissatisfied.

The level of dissatisfaction with the government's record and the high level of personal unpopularity enjoyed by the premier placed Liberal candidates in a difficult position. As the incumbent in Deux-Montages put it, 'During this present campaign all Liberal members are on their own.' Left on their own, the Liberal candidates attempted the tactics of disassociation. In the Gaspé and the eastern townships, along the north shore and around Lac St Jean the Liberals ignored independence and Bourassa and talked about forestry and agriculture, aid to the farmer, and the Alcan strike. In Kamouraska-Temiscouta party workers removed the 'Non au separatisme' from the top of the party signs. (A Bourassa aide admitted that several ridings had been given permission to cut out the slogan if it was irrelevant in the local contest.) However, the local candidates were vulnerable not only because they had just enjoyed six years in office, but also because many of them simply did not have the personal ability upon which to fall back. Without the force from the centre many Liberal campaigns collapsed.

The Parti québécois took the offensive from the outset with each local campaign finely tuned to local issues. In the urban areas the emphasis was on housing, public transportation, the provision of health and other services (particularly for the elderly), pollution, and high unemployment. For the Montreal area the PQ presented a comprehensive policy paper – 'Pour une nouvelle politique montréalaise' ('Towards a new policy for Montreal') – recommending massive decentralization in decision-making, low-cost housing, a revitalized public transportation system, and a public inquiry into the cost of the Olympics. It was not difficult to find the local issues in the Saguenay – Lac St Jean area. The three issued, as *La Presse* noted, were 'Alcan ... Alcan ... Alcan.' Out of work for six months the residents of four of the five ridings had little patience for talk about the economic consequences of independence. Dozens of other prolonged strikes throughout the province – in Drummond, Richelieu, Beauharnois, Chaveau, Lévis, Louis-Hébert (where a strike of professors left thousands of students free all term to campaign for Claude Morin), Kamouraska, and Montreal's south shore (where a six-month strike of suburban bus drivers caused traffic nightmares) – created solid local issues for the PQ to exploit. The closing of some industries – in Matane and Ste Anne – and soaring unemployment – in Duplessis, the Gaspé, Rivière du Loup, and Montreal's east end – provided ample local issues in other urban and semi-urban ridings.

The most important single issue in rural Quebec was the federal milk quota policy. Dairy farmers around Lac St Jean, along the south shore of the St Lawrence, throughout the eastern townships, and the southwest were enraged by a policy that was supposed to have cost them $40 million. Despite the last minute $22 million subsidy from the Bourassa government it was likely that most of the eighty-seven thousand dairy farmers would express their discontent in a more consequential manner than painting angry slogans on their barns. 'The federal government's milk policy certainly didn't help us in the rural areas,' the premier admitted when it was all over and the Liberals were wiped out in agricultural Quebec. But the milk quota issue was not the only one effectively used by the opposition. Both the PQ and the Union nationale promised a new deal for the farmer, and the PQ promised the development of a better rural roads network and the improvement in rural social and public services. Péquiste candidates also promised that their government would pay more attention to the primary sector, and exert greater control over industry in the workers' interest.

Clearly if elections, like football games, were won in the line the Liberals were in trouble.

The pre-election polls all reported a large number of undecided, and if the editorial writers did not share that indecision they had considerable difficulty rationalizing their choice. In a front-page editorial in the Montreal *Gazette* (November 13) publisher Ross Munro warned that the central issue was separation and regardless of the promised referendum a PQ victory would set in motion a process that would ruin Quebec economically and ultimately destroy the country. 'It is to be hoped that voters will take into consideration these factors and remember when they go to the polling booths that there are federal options open to them,' he wrote without indicating a preference. 'If they exercise these options in ridings where it would count, they will avoid blundering in a direction they don't want to go.' On the editorial page, however, the *Gazette* realized that voting the federalist option in most ridings meant voting Liberal, but 'we would be doing so in the knowledge that the Liberals were getting their comeuppance elsewhere ... ' The paper had little patience with the Bourassa campaign theme, and commented that 'It is futile, however, to wave the bogey of a vote against the Liberals as a vote for separatism in front of people who know it is not so. Voters are not cannon fodder to be fired against the ruling party's opponents.' Much the same view was shared by anglophone radio stations CJAD and CKGM.

The *Montreal Star* and station CFCF were not prepared to let their criticism of the Bourassa government stand in the way of recommending a solid Liberal vote. But it was agonizing to have to put it down in cold black type:

'Mr. Lévesque is the most attractive political leader; Mr. Biron of the Union Nationale has shown himself to be possessed of an engaging common sense, which is refreshing on a political platform; Mr. Bourassa, except on rare occasions, has seemed to be both defensive and inconclusive in his discussion of political problems. He has not, however, been hesitant on where he stands on the central issue of Canada. Neither, of course, has Mr. Biron, but his chances of winning this election are very slim.

'The choice will be frustrating for many, but it is not a choice for which the Liberals are responsible, it is essentially a choice determined by the Parti québécois. To help that party obtain office on the assumption that minds can be changed in time for the referendum, ignores the effects of the period between election and referendum which are bound to be substantial and essentially negative.

'Mr. Bourassa should realize, however, and his party also, that many will support him despite any doubt they may have. The massive electoral victory in 1973 did not produce the kind of government the voters are entitled to expect, nor, from the minority point of view, the kind of response an important segment of the province should receive.'

At *La Presse* two editorial writers and publisher Roger Lemelin surveyed the scene and came out reluctantly for the Liberals. Writing on October 30, Ivan Guay declared bluntly that referendum tactic was 'the worst kind of opportunism ... By trying to play the chameleon the PQ has disqualified itself as a serious alternative to the Liberal party. For it can't make us forget the fact that it is separatist before anything else. The PQ should either be frankly and solely separatist or else publicly disavow its separatist choice if it intends to portray itself as the alternative to the party in office. It cannot honourably play both parts at once.' In a final election-eve editorial on November 13, Mr. Guay attacked both parties for not dealing with the basic problems of the economy. On the contrary, he wrote, they 'have assumed that the voters are like hungry fish, and they need only lower the bait of allowances and subsidies to get them on to their hooks. In this sense, the election campaign now drawing to its close is not only following the venerable tradition of unrealistic promises, but is actually doing it one better as both parties proclaim their faith in the virtues of the welfare state.' But to deal with the fundamental economic problems and remove unemployment and inflation it was important to know that Quebec rested on Canadian and foreign economies and had more need of Canada than the reverse. 'The citizens must be aware of these facts,' he emphasized. 'And this is why it will take no small degree of discernment on Monday for them to prove their political maturity. For the propaganda of the parties is the antithesis of any reasonably impartial economic analysis!'

Marcel Adam found the PQ position on the referendum unacceptable and ambiguous. The idea of a referendum, he wrote: 'is really a snare for the voter, a federalists-dissatisfied-with-the-outgoing-government trap, since it does not involve asking the Québécois whether or not they want Quebec's separation before the independentist process is unleashed, but simply requesting a stronger mandate if Ottawa says no.

'In this respect we may wonder how candid the PQ is being, for in promising to pass an act to affirm Quebec's independence immediately following the election it apparently thinks it will have been authorized to do so by victory at the polls. Why a referendum in case of trouble, then? It must be one thing or the other: either, realizing that an election resulting in the overthrow of power has a bit of everything but especially general dissatisfaction with the outgoing government, the PQ accepts that success at the polls will not have given it a clear mandate to proceed with independence; or else its only aim in promising a referendum is to attract the votes of a non-separatist clientele needed to get it into office, and unobtainable without this dangerous ploy.

'I call this dangerous since a possible Péquiste government would so need the massive support of the Québécois in bargaining with Ottawa that it must not get into an untenable position; and this is what will happen if its success can be attributed to a calculated misunderstanding which induced many people to give it their support without proper knowledge of the facts.

'The party that has promised to do everything to achieve independence as harmoniously as possible owes this candour to the Québécois. If the PQ believes that Quebec has been cheated in Confederation, it should not attempt to get it out by cheating the Québécois itself.'

The fundamental issue, the only issue, concluded Adam, was: 'should Quebec remain in Confederation or not?' 'To the undecided voters who simply want a change of government in the name of healthy democratic turn-taking, we can suggest that they ask themselves a different question: is it appropriate to break up a country to get rid of an unsatisfactory government?' (*La Presse*, November 9)

A day later Adam compared independence and association to the young husband who divorced his wife and having experienced 'the exorbitantly expensive pleasure of a certain emancipation' remarried the same woman. Without absolving the government of its many failures, 'which are so numerous and which I have often deplored,' he argued that federalism was not the principal cause of Quebec's difficulties but that it was 'necessary, in fact, to realize that Quebec is one of the most difficult western societies to govern because of its cultural situation, geography, and extraordinary economy.' But, he admitted, circumstances since 1973 gave the dissatisfied federalist only a choice between cholera and the plague.

There was more to the Parti québécois than the simple advocacy of independence, he continued, on November 11. The PQ stood for three revolutionary changes: independence, á republican system, and a social democratic state. After examining the implications of each he asked: 'Consider our economic stagnation, our democratic under-de-velopment, the meagre sense of social responsibility among our inter-est groups, the rebellious mood in the unions, the little respect shown the law by those who should be enforcing it and those who should be obeying it, the triumph of egotistical interests over the common inter-est; consider all this and then agree that before building tomorrow's society we must first make a success of the society of today. No one becomes a patron or a philanthropist without first being successful at money and life.

"One can try grafting socialism on to a society in the midst of eco-nomic and democratic development such as our own, but this would be dictatorship and not democracy. Without being sure what that would give us, we do know what it takes away.

'At a time when Quebec is still coping with the after-effects of the quiet revolution, which was timid by comparison with what the PQ wants to do, and is still trying, after a decade, to repair the great re-forms that miscarried; when all Quebec wants is to absorb tranquilly the effects of dizzying social change and try to decide whether change is always synonymous with progress, are we wise to involve it simultaneously in three revolutionary reforms ?'

Publisher Roger Lemelin delivered the final charge in a November 13 front-page editorial: 'Even in these columns M. Bourassa has come under frank criticism for his leadership style. Yet a sense of fair play obliges us to resist the wave of frenzy that has risen against him. M. Bourassa is an honest man and a good democrat. He stands up to the implacable M. Trudeau. The unfortunate strikes in the public sector found him flexible, calm, firm. Foreign investors trust him. He has a thorough knowledge of his business. He has health, youth, and endur-ance going for him. His colleagues and the general public have fre-quently been irritated by the convolutions of his style of government and his tendency to leave problems and crises to fester. Yet a tougher and more direct man might have turned these crises into violent and bloody confrontations of the kind we have not seen in Quebec for six years under M. Bourassa. Let it be said frankly: for some years, we in Quebec have been given a first taste of the destruction of a society that took us three hundred years to build. The agitators who want this eruption have also been irritated and hamstrung by M. Bourassa's elu-sive style, checking and restraining them.

'For the most part wrongly, M. Bourassa is made the scapegoat for all the frustrations of the public. If he stays in office he will see his majority considerably reduced, and this will be so much the better. A democratic government is as strong as the quality and numbers of its opposition. Moreover the lesson administered by the voters may finally prompt him to improve, and seek the breadth expected of a statesman in Quebec ... In short, the Liberal party gives us a *status quo* that excites no one, but it will be the choice of those for whom discretion is placed ahead of all other feelings, and ahead of the taste for adventure.

'The more aware of their identity the French population of Quebec becomes, the more impatient they are with the yoke of Canadian federalism, whose efficiency can only work against the national enthusiasm of the Québécois. Quebec is part of a whole from which it differs in language, culture, and temperament.

'All Québécois are deeply pained by this compromise, accepted for the sake of our economic security on a continent where we are isolated geographically and culturally. All those for whom the passion of nationality takes precedence over practical considerations have found an ideal catalyst in René Lévesque. Intelligent, disorganized, idealistic, an unrivalled communicator, attractive but undisciplined, he unites powerfully in himself the sincerest qualities and aspirations of French-Canadian nationalism. In his party, unhappily, he also shelters radical and anarchical factions that moved in to use it for their own dismal purposes and dream of getting rid of M. Lévesque at the earliest opportunity. Up to now he has neutralized them, and thus done a service to Quebec.

'The PQ comes to the voters laden with debt. M. Lévesque has been made to say 'no' to separatism. He thus escapes from his own internal dilemma (posed by the unconditional separatists) by wishing it on the voters in the form of the fallacious referendum. In order to restrain the extremist factions in his party he plies us with a social-democratic platform by which Quebec would turn into a super-bureaucracy administering wonderful social-assistance programmes that would crush us with taxes, do profound injury to our individual freedoms, and make the working class the first victim of his crazy adventure. When one considers that the already-existing social-assistance programmes in Canada and Quebec are beyond our means and are in large part responsible for inflation, it is sheer madness to want to increase them. This economic angelism, whose doleful consequences for Quebec M. Lévesque has not outlined, makes one's flesh creep.

'Are we to prefer survival, constricted but still breathing, within the

Canadian federation, to brutal strangulation at the hands of a half-baked Quebec socialism? This is a painful question to ask just now: the Péquistes are in the grip of an enthusiastic frenzy that is something to see, but at the same time their majority is afflicted with that kind of deafness which can but will not hear. It is possible to be a good Québécois without being a Péquiste, and the political duty of a good Québécois is to point out the dangers weighing on our economic system, which has contributed to our survival as a French people.

'At all events, if M. Lévesque is kept in opposition despite his popularity among a noisy and active portion of the electorate, it will be because of the ambiguities in his election platform, his camouflage of separatism, his economic angelism, his camouflage of the socialism that has always been the real thrust of his political thinking and which he can realize only in a separate Quebec, and because of the differences weakening his party, not because of the nasty middle class or the nasty federalists ...

'Yes, the voter is in a terrible fix. In this beautiful land, where it is still a fine thing to live in freedom, he has to choose between a tiresome *status quo* and a rollicking embarcation, despite bad weather, in the European-style social-democrat dory outward bound for Percé Rock.

'Think carefully, and vote on Monday!'

But there was far more interest in the position Claude Ryan, editor of *Le Devoir*, would take. An ultra-nationalist who had in the past come down on the side of a vastly decentralized federal system, Mr. Ryan began his lengthy journey in a November 12 editorial. He found the Liberal economic record better than many and argued that, given the 'extremely strong and conflicting currents' through which he had to navigate, Bourassa's labour policy was better than his critics on the left and the right allowed. But he believed that the premier had lost his dynamism, even his conviction, perhaps even his courage; had placed party before country when ethics were involved; and had earned his unpopularity 'by the often zigzagging and calculating leadership he had displayed. The Parti québécois, while not perfect, 'far from it' (particularly because 40 per cent of its candidates were teachers and professors), was the most democratic and financially open, had a 'remarkable dynamic' leader, possessed the confidence of the young, had a team capable of governing the province, and offered 'a noble vision of what public life should be in Quebec.' After twelve years of Liberal governments since 1960, Mr. Ryan concluded, a change would be in order, 'if only the objection of their commitment to independence can be separated out in a loyal and satisfactory way.'

The second editorial on November 13 turned to independence and the referendum. Ryan noted that the PQ had concentrated on economic and social questions and had insisted that independence was not the issue in the campaign: 'To any honest man, this line the PQ has taken in the campaign amounts to a genuine moral commitment to do nothing that would set Quebec irrevocably on the road to separation until the question is referred in plain terms to the judgment of the people. Yet this is not quite what we read in some highly explicit passages of the PQ platform. From this document we learn in fact that a Péquiste government would be bound to 'set in motion immediately the process of accession to sovereignty by bringing before the National Assembly, shortly after its election, a bill authorizing it to demand from Ottawa the repatriation of all powers to Quebec and, to this end, enter into technical discussions with Ottawa on the transfer of jurisdiction.'

'In the case of a refusal from Ottawa, the PQ clearly promises a referendum. Equally, it is committed to submit a draft constitution to the people in due course. But chances are good that the crucial process would be under way well before we got to the stage of the referendum and referring the constitution to the public. The risk would be greater if the PQ gained office with an absolute majority of the seats.

'Especially in these last few days, there have been numerous attempts to get the PQ to clarify these crucial points. The farthest the PQ went in terms of clarification came Thursday and Friday evening of this week in television interviews given by M. Lévesque. In them he gave his assurance that no decision would be made precipitately and certainly none would be imposed on us; he guaranteed that any referendum would be held with a maximum of democratic precaution, he even promised that a first term of office would see only one referendum, and that a Péquiste government would consider itself bound by the results. Apart from the facts, however, that these promises are merely verbal and that they do seem occasionally to stretch the actual texts somewhat, they simply do not erase the perfectly clear passages I have cited from the Péquiste platform.

'Those who insist on seeing guarantees confirmed in official documents will obviously not be satisfied by the clarification the PQ has offered. No union dealing with an employer on a contract that is to embody firm guarantees is going to accept simple verbal commitments. Why should a citizen who insists on voting in this spirit not do the same?

The question was left unanswered, and Mr. Ryan concluded that in any event it was important that the federalist option should be strongly represented in the Assembly and therefore voters with 'federalist convictions' should have no hesitation in voting Liberal when the Liberal candidates were clearly superior to those of the PQ.

The question of independence apparently 'put in parenthesis' Claude Ryan then returned to the obvious benefits of a PQ victory.

'Beyond the judicial aspects of a possible PQ victory, there are the political aspects. At this level, a PQ win would have definite effects that could not be minimized. These could even, some think, make up for the absence of specific guarantees mentioned a little while back. Thus:

'1 Internally, a change of government would mark the start of an intensive movement of political and social renewal. M. Bourassa has chosen to stress the economic and financial risks accompanying such a change. On the other hand the PQ, being closer to union and intellectual circles as well as the younger generation, might plausibly find it easier, at least for a time, to foster a climate of greater confidence in our institutions and public men. This is what Quebec most needs at the present time. In fact the stability that should come from this improved atmosphere is a prerequisite for the revival of an economy deeply disturbed by the weakening of leadership we have observed in recent years.

'2 Outside Quebec M. Lévesque's impact, as I have already stressed, is much greater than M. Bourassa's. If he were put in office Ottawa would be forced at last to open its eyes, and, after the countless denials of recent years, admit there was in truth a big problem in Quebec. This admission could be followed by some specific proposals such as we have been demanding for almost fifteen years. It might signal a thaw that could lead eventually for a novel solution, neither the *status quo* nor the total, brutal separation rejected by the large majority of Québécois.

'For English Canada the return of a Péquiste government would come as a beneficial shock. They would realize once and for all that the problem of two nations was not something created solely by what the historian Donald Creighton has recently dubbed the travelling salesmen of bilingualism and biculturalism. What might come from this is a much more favourable atmosphere for candid bargaining than the secret conventicles of the premiers.

'At all events, a Péquiste win would force supporters of each of the two theories to burnish up their weapons for a decisive confrontation. This may be our first chance to get to the bottom of a problem that politicians have always used for election purposes without once looking at it really closely.

'If we elect a Péquiste government on Monday we take the chance of later being drawn into a gamble the result of which is unknown, though for the moment the mere principle is distasteful to a majority of citizens. Two factors offset the risk, however:

'1 A Péquiste government would be obliged to function in the Canadian constitutional framework or else expect the penalties prescribed for those who break the law;

'2 It would also be bound by the very powerful moral commitments made publicly in the election campaign.

'If we elect a Liberal government we would be reaffirming the Québécois' support for federalism, but we would also be getting Quebec deeper into political stagnation and the shabby balancing acts that are diametrically opposed to true political life. We would be giving credibility to the politics of those who think elections can still be won by fear. If we defeat the Liberals, we also force them to a thorough review of their leadership and goals in anticipation of the toughest confrontations Quebec will ever have seen.

'Of these risks we must choose the one that does more to open the door to the future.'

The *Globe* reported much of the editorial under the cut line '*Le Devoir* leans toward the PQ but doesn't go all the way.' But André Beliveau of *La Presse* was much closer to the truth when he exclaimed, 'Spectacular about-face at *Le Devoir*: M. Claude Ryan supports the Parti québécois.'

Both the Liberals and the Péquistes were cautious in their predictions. When the campaign ended the Liberals believed they would win at least 40 per cent of the vote and sixty-eight seats. Privately, it was reported, the Péquistes were expecting to win about 40 per cent of the vote and anywhere from thirty to seventy seats depending on the regional breakdown. Very few political speculators saw a wide margin of victory for either party, and most settled uncomfortably on the side of a small Liberal majority, a Liberal or PQ minority government.

The opinion polls, however, were unanimous and emphatic in the over-all supremacy of the Parti québécois, and had been throughout the year as the table shows.

Voting intentions 1976

	Lib	PQ	UN	Créd.	PNP	Others	?
April	21.5	31.6	7.6	6.9	9.8		22.7
(CROP)							
May	23	30	6	6	4	1	31
(Gallup)							
September	23.4	29.4	12.2	12.2	5.1		20.1
(CROP-Libs)							
Oct. 25-31	22.8	31.3	10.5	3.1	1.6	.09	29.7
(CROP)							
Nov. 1-5	15.9	29.5	8.4	3.6	1	1.2	40.5*
(INCI)							

*30 undecided, 6 refuse to respond, and 4.5 not to vote.

With the undecided distributed in the November 1-5 poll, conducted by Maurice Pinard and Richard Hamilton of McGill, the PQ led the Liberals 50 to 27 per cent. In percentage of the total vote their lead was overwhelmingly in Montreal East (69 to 19), Montreal region (50 to 32), Quebec area (51 to 25), Saguenay – North shore (58 to 29), the St Maurice (47 to 26), and even in the eastern townships (43 to 23). However, most observers believed that the undistributed would not distribute themselves as had the decided but would tend to waver towards the Liberals and with the exception of Montreal east were not prepared to predict a PQ sweep of most of the province.

The verdict

During the day a record of over 85 per cent of the voters had gone to the polls and by 8:30 at night the computer predicted a majority PQ government. Less than two hours later, as his own seat swung in the balance, Premier Bourassa conceded defeat. When the final returns were all in – including a December 23 recount in Hull – René Lévesque's Parti québécois had swept francophone Quebec and won seventy-one seats with 41.4 per cent of the vote. From 102 seats in 1973 the Liberals had fallen to twenty-six, and among the defeated were the premier and many of his most prominent cabinet ministers. To the surprise of most observers Rodrigue Biron and Liberal mismanagement had brought the UN back from near oblivion with eleven seats and 18.2 per cent of the vote.

The Parti québécois had increased in strength in every region of

the province, including western Montreal. The gains were most striking east of Quebec on both sides of the river where they added about
16 per cent of the popular vote. The party dominated urban and semi-
urban Quebec, except for the non-francophone ridings in Montreal,
and made strong inroads into the rural areas. The Liberals, on the
other hand, were almost reduced to an anglophone rump as far as
seats were concerned. Fourteen of their twenty-six seats were in
Montreal West where there was a majority of anglophone voters in
eight ridings and over 36 per cent in the rest. Outside of Montreal the
party held Pontiac which was about 60 per cent anglophone, and Ar-
genteuil and Gatineau both of which were about 30 per cent non-francophone. Four of the remaining nine seats were won by less than one
thousand votes. Only Gérard Lévesque in Bonaventure and Raymond
Garneau in Jean Talon, and the ridings of Charlevoix, Portneuf, and
Montmagny were firmly in the Liberal camp, and even there the margins dropped dramatically.

Popular Vote: 1976 preliminary complete figures
(1973 results in parentheses)

	Vote	% of votes	Seats
PQ	1,390,363	41.4 (30.3)	71 (6)
Lib.	1,134,997	33.8 (54.8)	26 (102)
UN	611,678	18.2 (4.9)	11 (0)
PC	155,508	4.6 (9.9)	1 (2)
Other	67,681	2.0	1 (0)

Popular vote by region 1976

Region	Total vote	% Lib	% PQ	% UN	% PC	% other	Seats
Montreal Region	750,603	31.13	45.14	19.7	3.83	0.24	21
Montreal East	591,370	33.02	52.04	11.23	2.35	1.36	18
Montreal West	502,768	43.78	26.34	22.03	1.26	6.59	16
Quebec City	155,474	37.33	48.48	10.27	3.56	0.36	5
Quebec Region	330,450	35.30	36.84	17.33	4.86	5.66	11
Three Rivers	169,071	29.72	39.96	24.01	5.79	0.52	6
Eastern Twps.	295,699	27.01	33.41	31.36	7.81	0.41	11
Ottawa Region and North West	186,773	33.87	33.65	15.50	16.41	0.56	7
Saguenay–Lac St Jean	208,715	27.83	54.39	11.17	5.70	0.92	7
Lower St Lawrence–Gaspe	169,304	35.31	42.22	16.63	5.61	0.24	8

Source: Rapport Préliminaire: Elections Générales du 15 Novembre 1976

Linguistically it was clear that francophone Quebec had cast a majority vote for the PQ. The November Pinard-Hamilton poll indicated that 54 per cent of the French Canadians polled intended to vote PQ, 26 per cent Liberal, and 14 per cent UN. English Canadians split 11, 31, and 49 per cent for the PQ, Liberals and UN respectively. Thirty-one per cent of the new Canadians indicated a preference for the PQ, while 30 per cent intended to vote for the Liberals and the same percentage Union nationale. Francophone support for the PQ was the highest in Montreal East with 73 per cent, compared to 53 per cent in the west end and 50 per cent elsewhere in the province. Pierre Champagne, a mathematician with an interest in election analysis, estimated that 64 per cent of the francophones in the Montreal East ridings and 57.5 per cent in northern Montreal voted PQ. In greater Montreal, he concluded, the PQ won all ridings that were more than 64 per cent francophone and the Liberals and UN won those which were more than 63 per cent anglophone (*La Presse*, December 9).

Before the election there were indications that anglophones and new Canadians would vote for the UN in protest against the language provisions of Bill 22, and the Pinard-Hamilton survey indicated that 49 per cent in greater Montreal planned to vote UN. Anger obviously subsided on the way to the polling booth, but there was a very large UN vote in the overwhelmingly anglophone ridings in western Montreal. Pointe-Claire went to the UN, the first time in history that an anglophone riding had voted UN. In Jacques-Cartier, about 50 per cent non-francophone, the Liberal Noël St-Germain edged James Carter, the UN candidate, by only 1,255 votes, as the UN increased Its vote from 705 in 1973 to over nine thousand. In Marguerite-Bourgeoys, Fernand Lalonde, who had considered moving to a safer riding, saw his plurality fall to 806 votes over the PQ as Domenico Izzi secured over ten thousand votes for the UN.

In twelve ridings the increase in the UN vote since 1973 was greater than the difference between the victorious PQ and the defeated Liberal. Four were in Montreal, and all had significant non-francophone minorities. In many of the ten in the Montreal region there was also a significant ethnic minority vote, as there was in Papineau. When the renegade Liberal George Springate only held Westmount with 8,700 votes to almost 6,000 for the UN and 4,500 for Nick auf der Maur there could be little doubt that in greater Montreal, the eastern townships, and the Ottawa valley the non-francophones registered a massive protest against the Bourassa government. *La Presse* had estimated on October 16 that a slight shift of the non-francophone vote away from the Liberals in ten Montreal ridings could give the seat to the Parti québécois, including Bourassa's Mercier. In the end all ten ridings went PQ, although there was clearly a massive switch of the French-Canadian voter as well as a likely change in anglophone and ethnic allegiance.

As well as being the likely cause of Liberal defeats in a dozen ridings, the Union nationale also won ten seats from the Liberals. Generally the party won in the areas of its traditional strength along the south shore and in the eastern townships. They also came second in thirteen ridings, six of them in western Montreal. Rodrigue Biron had no difficulty winning Lotbinière with a solid majority. Fabien Roy of the PNP held his fortress of Beauce-sud with three times the vote of his Liberal opponent, but Camille Samson was pressed by the Parti québécois in Rouyn-Noranda.

Clearly the verdict was a striking defeat of the Liberals and an equally categorical vote of confidence in René Lévesque and the PQ. Equally clearly not even the most ardent Péquiste argued that it was a vote for independence. The pre-election Pinard-Hamilton poll had surveyed opinion on independence. Eighteen per cent favoured independence and 58 per cent were opposed, while 24 per cent were undecided or refused to answer. However, the linguistic and regional breakdown was more interesting.

| | ILES DE MONTRÉAL ET JESUS: | | | | REST OF PROVINCE | |
| | East | | West | | | |
	Francophones	Others	Francophones	Others	Francophones	Others
In favour	30	6	24	8	18	12
Not in favour	45	78	57	79	56	79
Undecided No response	26	17	19	13	26	10
Number of Respondents	132	18	89	77	733	42

The poll also revealed that 49 per cent of those who intended to vote PQ favoured independence, and six per cent of the Liberals and 5 per cent of the UN supporters did so as well. Twenty-six per cent of those who intended to vote PQ opposed independence and 24 per cent were undecided. Support for independence was strongest among the eighteen to twenty-four age group with 29 per cent in favour, and among those with over fourteen years of school with 33 per cent supporting independence.

Clearly the two step approach to independence allowed some federalists to vote for the Parti québécois. But it was also clear, though not statistically, that separatism had ceased to frighten the voter. Since 1973 the party had clearly been able to break the connection many voters still drew between independence and violence; it had also successfully neutralized the extremists on the nationalist and social front. It was possible, as a result, for the Quebec voter to take his chances on the future, feeling as did both Jean Marchand and Marc Lalonde that they could live in an independent Quebec much the same as in a Canadian province. Psychologically, at least, the province had taken a giant step towards independence; for the first time it was clear that independence was regarded as one of the rational and legitimate options open to the Québécois. Neither the province nor the country could ever be quite the same again.

Epilogue

Towards independence *and* association?

By the end of 1976 Canadians had learned to live with the Parti québécois. The shock of November 15 had been absorbed: the call of the
Toronto Star and Dalton Camp for a national government had gone
unheeded; the stock market had recovered; the prime minister promised that force would never be used to keep Quebec in Canada and
urged all Canadians to do their bit by supporting bilingualism; and
René Lévesque and his cabinet went about governing their domain.
With Parizeau and Tremblay in finance and industry it was clear that
domestic policies would be moderate. And at the party's annual convention on December 18 the premier urged the rank and file to start
preparing for the referendum – and let the government govern. For
the moment, at least, a clash between the party militants and the government was avoided, as the premier gently reminded the convention
that the government had to be that of all Quebeckers, not just of the
PQ, and had to be free to act on its own initiative.

The goal of independence remained, but the word 'separatism' was
struck from the party vocabulary. The goal was independence *and*
association, however, and it was clear that 'association' would be
equally emphasized as the government began to prepare for the referendum. In Ottawa at the first ministers conference on December 13
Premier Lévesque explained the nature of the new game and its rules
to his colleagues:

'We have stated clearly, and I wish to repeat it, that we do not claim
to see this vote as a mandate for Quebec's independence. Our commitments are clear on this point: when the time comes, it will be up to

the public, and to them alone, to decide the issue in a referendum.

'But it would take minds set in an unbending view of political reality not to see that there has been an extremely rapid change in Quebec society. Quebec has been engaged for the last fifteen years in redefining itself as a community and, therefore, its relationship with others.

'This redefinition began and is gathering momentum through what are essential democratic means, chief among which has been the founding, development and now the coming to power of a party which has never hidden its true colours on the basic issues.

'Such a dynamic development obviously has caused and still does cause some apprehension, especially to those who do not understand it. But it now appears to be irreversible.

'For this reason, without taking too much of the time of this conference, I feel I must take advantage of my first opportunity to address the political leaders of the federation, to ask that they, and all Canadians, understand the development of Quebec and the positive spirit in which we see the future of our relations taking shape.

'In no way do we see these relations in the perspective of recurrent confrontations which have become more or less that of the present system and which too frequently produce hostility out of misunderstanding.

'On the contrary, it is precisely in order to do away with this confrontation once and for all that we propose not to destroy, but to adjust, the political institutions to the dynamic reality of Quebec as well as to the true Canadian reality.

'We are indeed convinced that the new type of relations we envisaged and which we will reformulate at the appropriate time will improve matters not only for us but also for all our neighbours because it will be more consistent with the deep and normal leanings of our societies.

'We believe that Canada and English-speaking Canadians are capable of accepting such a perspective that would make it possible in a different setting not to isolate ourselves from each other, nor to continue to harass each other with artificial issues like bilingualism, but rather to differentiate political institutions which should be different, while maintaining and even expanding all types of co-operation and exchanges that are mutually beneficial to us. We are certain that the development of Quebec, like that of Canada, clearly depends on this.'

The dialogue within Quebec and with Canadians had begun. The strategy of René Lévesque was clear. What was not clear was whether the coalition of forces and the leadership would be found in Quebec to advocate the federalist position. If not, independence *and* association, so gently argued, could easily win the day.